Northern New York

D1500756

Northern New York

Cheri Revai

North Country Books, Inc.
Utica, New York

Weird Northern New York
Copyright © 2006
by Cheri Revai

Design by Zach Steffen & Rob Igoe Jr.

ISBN 1-59531-012-6

Library of Congress Cataloging-in-Publication Data

Revai, Cheri, 1963-
Weird northern New York / by Cheri Revai.
p. cm.
Includes bibliographical references.
ISBN 1-59531-012-6 (alk. paper)
1. Haunted places--New York (State) 2. Ghosts--New York (State) I. Title.
BF1472.U6R482 2006
130.9747'5--dc22
2006030099

Cover Photos:
The Spicer home. Photo by Stephanie Demers. Courtesy of M. Spicer
Gruesome discovery. Courtesy of *Adirondack Album—Volume Two* by Barney Fowler
42-point buck. Courtesy of *Adirondack Album—Volume Two* by Barney Fowler

North Country Books, Inc.
311 Turner Street
Utica, New York 13501
www.northcountrybooks.com

I dedicate "Weird" to my wonderful brother, Tom Dishaw.

Contents

Introduction

Tell people you're writing a book called *Weird Northern New York*, and you're bound to get a lot of raised eyebrows. Luckily, I've had a lot of experience with such mildly amused expressions the past six years, so it doesn't faze me. When I wrote my first book, *Haunted Northern New York*, in 2000, some people asked me if the stories were made up and if I really believed in "that stuff." (Answers: No and yes, respectively.) Ghosts and haunted houses, it seems, still carry some sort of archaic stigma of being either blasphemous and evil or pure science fiction. In fact, at one privately-owned bookstore I visited in the Plattsburgh area hoping to find additional sources of information on local ghosts and such, I was directed to the "Science Fiction" section by an employee— and he did it with the utmost seriousness. This is not science fiction, folks. It's paranormal, it's supernatural, it's extraordinary, and it's weird, if you will—but it's not science fiction. Science fiction is "literary fantasy involving the imagined impact of science on society," according to the online Princeton University source, *WordNet 2.0*. Two little words in that definition don't belong in this book: fantasy and imagined.

On the other hand, "Weird" means "suggestive of the preternatural or supernatural; of a strikingly odd or unusual character; strange," according to *The American Heritage College Dictionary, Third Edition*. Now we're on the same page. You're going to be seeing a lot of the word "weird" in this book. Ghost stories are and always have been "weird," by the very definition of that word, so I've included quite a few new ones in *Weird Northern New York*; most notably, a lengthy story about our local ghost hunters—the Shadow Chasers—who investigate college campuses, graveyards, private residences, and public facilities with an abundance of technical gadgets you'd love to get your hands on. There are also stories about ghosts that haunt Crane School of Music students, patrons at a local hotel, a mountain lake, and a resort. And there is the ghost with a penchant for electronics, a ghost that sneezes to make itself known, and ghosts that have commandeered the stairways of private homes. But there's so much more that's truly weird than just ghosts to talk about…

There is the stone fetus and the oldest person alive, both in Herkimer County; a hapless hermit from the Town of Hammond, as well as the most famous hermit of all from the Adirondacks; earthquakes, devastating wind sheers, and even a year without a summer; hangings, murders, and amazing feats of accomplishment; and eccentrics both wealthy and poor. There have been secret societies, blood libel, and mob mentality; tiny dinosaur-like beings, early unknown explorers who left their mark in stone, and giant river creatures. We had a "lady in the lake" whose preserved remains were discovered thirty years after she was drowned; a man who went deep into the woods of Essex County, chained himself to trees with padlocks, and threw away the keys; and a record-breaking forty-two-point buck. And there was the unusual bounty hunt law of 1871 to exterminate all wolves and panthers from the Adirondacks, because their numbers were too large; the mysterious floating islands phenomena at Higley Flow; and the vortex at Thompson Park, which caused several people to vanish and reappear elsewhere.

Northern New York has always been a region at odds with itself—a place where conservationists are pitted against modern urbanites in an ongoing battle for prime Adirondack property and undeveloped North Country farmlands. The one wants to keep it all as is, with no further destruction in the name of "progress"; and the other wants to exploit our natural resources for the economic value of tourism and recreation. Even residents of the North Country are at odds with themselves. Edward Litchfield, for example, who loved to hunt native species so much that, when wolves and panthers were brought to the brink of extinction by the bounty law, he left the area. But then he returned several years later and bought thousands of acres of Adirondack property so he could create his very own wild game preserve. He stocked his preserve with both exotic and native species with the intent of restoring wildlife, at least in his little part of the world. Yet, his sole purpose of restoring animals to the wild was so he had something to hunt—making him both pro animal preservation and pro hunting at the same time. And what about the one and only Noah John Rondeau— the late, great Adirondack hermit? Toward the end of his life, he had to give up his hermitage and return to society, where he told the world about the Adirondacks and their beauty, as well as his life as a hermit. He went from shunning society to almost embracing it—a very un-hermit-like thing to do; but it was necessary, and he was right to do it for the good of all.

Yale's secret society, the Order of Skull and Bones, owns a private island on the St. Lawrence River near Alexandria Bay. All Bonesmen, including President George Bush and Senator John Kerry, have visited the island at least once, if only as a token gesture. Not a big deal. But did you know that much previously secret information about Skull and Bones has come to light recently, like the fact that Bonesmen are taught that they are Knights and all outsiders (like you and me) are Barbarians? And because they put themselves above and ahead of the rest of us, the clocks in their meeting house—the Tomb at Yale University—are always set five minutes fast as a reminder. Most alarming are the rituals and artifacts Bonesmen have used for years—many with ties to Nazi Germany and the concentration camps. Talk about being at odds with one's self. Everything Skull and Bones initiates are told to embrace their senior year at Yale, especially their "holier than thou" attitude, seems unbecoming for men of such esteem who, these days, thank goodness, embrace the public with a much different attitude—especially if they want to keep their voters.

Even Mother Nature is at odds with herself here in the North Country. We may not get hurricanes or tropical storms this far north, but we get unforgettable ice storms, devastating winds, mini-tornadoes, earthquakes, and even years with no summer. So, as far as weather anomalies go, we've pretty much seen everything. In fact, as far as all kinds of anomalies and strange phenomena go, we've seen it all. I'm going to go out on a limb here and say that the North Country may well be the weirdest region around, bearing in mind all that the word "weird" represents. And I say that with the greatest respect. After all, to paraphrase SUNY Canton's catch-phrase that I'm especially fond of: This is *my* Northern New York!

Bizarre Behavior

Silent Screams

Westport

"Then Jesus was led by the Spirit up into the desert to be tempted by the devil. After forty days and nights he was very hungry…Then the devil let him alone, and angels came to him and took care of him."

—Verses 1 and 11, Chapter 4, "Book of Matthew," New Testament

On May 24, 1975, state police at Westport in Essex County received a call at 1:30 A.M. to report a vagrant shuffling along the side of Route 9N, possibly armed. What they discovered that morning was beyond comprehension, even for a couple of seasoned troopers. A tall thin man wrapped in chains from head to toe appeared out of the darkness. He had long unkempt hair and a beard, his clothes were like rags, and he smelled of urine and sweat. There were heavy-duty chains around his ankles, his neck, his shoulders, and running helter-skelter under the layers of his clothing. One bloodied hand had a broken handcuff still attached to it. His voice was hoarse. It would soon be understood why.

The state police discovered that the man was a native of New York City with an extensive criminal record, both from the city and from around the North Country. Five years earlier, he had been charged with incest in the city. A year before that, he was charged with possession of a weapon, and just before he fled to northern New York, he had been charged with assault. Moving northward, he continued his life of crime. In Elizabethtown, he was arrested for hitchhiking and for a similar crime in the Town of Peru, and he had been charged with assault in Malone. In his own mind, he knew he had done wrong, at least in the eyes of God;

3

and something inside of him told him that years of being in and out of jail repeatedly was not enough punishment to clear his soul of his crimes. He was determined to atone for his sins before he died.

The man told investigators he had bound his own body in chains deep in the woods of Westport where nobody could hear or see him as a sort of self-penance to atone for his many sins. He had planned to fast for forty days and nights (like Jesus did in the "Book of Matthew"), and by securing himself to the trees and tossing away the keys, he would accomplish that goal. But he only lasted three days with the ravenous mosquitoes and hunger pangs—three days of screaming for help where nobody could possibly hear him—before a stone he grabbed finally smashed through the handcuffs on his wrist, setting him free from his self-imposed hell. That's when he stumbled out to the highway and was spotted by a passerby who phoned the police.

He could not be held; he had broken no laws. A mental health evaluation revealed that the man's symptoms included "indifference, withdrawal, delusions of persecution, omnipotence, and hallucinations," according to seasoned author and reporter Barney Fowler. And yet…he was not considered violent or dangerous, at least not to anyone other than himself. So, amazingly, the man who was clearly suicidal and had such a lengthy criminal background was released. Again. Over and over again in this man's life, he had broken laws and had now progressed to attempting to kill himself, all in a vain effort to receive help and (in his own words) "feel safe." And over and over again, he was simply allowed to slip through the cracks of the criminal justice and mental health systems, even after he told the Town Justice that the "next time" he would do it right—"it" being the forty-day fast in the woods. He promised he would go out in the woods again, but this time, he would chain himself up away from any loose rocks that he might grab in a moment of weakness to unbind himself. His vow to authorities went unacknowledged, just like his screams of agony in the woods days before.

Five months later, a hunter walking half a mile into the woods off the Northway in the Town of North Hudson stumbled upon a human skull, which he at first thought was a deer skull. The police were dispatched to the scene, and the memory of the "man in chains" in Westport quickly came back to haunt them, for further inspection of the immediate area

Courtesy of *Adirondack Album—Volume Two* by Barney Fowler

Photo of gruesome discovery

revealed legs chained to a tree (see photo above), clothes, cigarettes, matches, a blank writing tablet, pens, a duffel bag, canteens, plastic bags…and more chains. A metal detector found six keys eleven feet away from the body where they had been tossed by the deceased, to ensure there would be no turning back this time. Even though no identification was found with the remains—and the body was in an advanced state of decomposition—the size 13 shoes found bound to the tree were the size of their man's. The chains were like those they had seen five months earlier. It was déjà vu. Local investigators contacted the New York City Police Department and were told that the man in question had not been seen for several months. They obtained his dental chart and X-rays and forwarded them to a doctor in Elizabethtown, who made a positive identification.

Because the only relative that the police determined to be next of kin didn't want to claim the remains, the Marvin Funeral Home in Elizabethtown buried him, and Essex County paid for it. It was the sad ending for a man who wanted the devil to leave him alone, so the angels would come and take care of him.

Murder and Mayhem

Canton, Louisville, South Colton

The Court of Common Pleas (St. Lawrence County Court) opened for business in Ogdensburg on June 1, 1802, with the outspoken Judge Nathan Ford on the bench. But no business would be conducted that day, nor for the two days that followed, because the associate judges were three days late. When they finally did appear, the men blamed their delay on the primitive road conditions; after all, the county had only been formed several months earlier, and the newly-lain trails were not exactly easy to traverse. But, after three days of tapping his fingers on the table waiting, Ford—known for his crudeness—was not a very happy man. Pity the first criminal to be presented in his chambers. According to Evert's *History of St. Lawrence County, N.Y.*, that criminal was guilty of only minor offenses, but for punishment, Ford "banished him from the face of God's earth." And what exactly might that mean, you ask? When the hapless man looked up at the cranky old judge and asked where he should go, Ford, without hesitation, screamed, "To *Canada*, God damn you!" (Technically, Canada is still part of God's earth, but Ford's options were apparently quite limited, and that was the first place that came to mind; Siberia being nearly impossible to get to from here in those days.)

* * *

Six men were hanged for murder by the St. Lawrence County sheriff between 1816 and 1898, when that form of capital punishment was replaced by the electric chair in the State Prison system. The gallows for all but the first hanging, which took place in Ogdensburg before the courthouse relocated to Canton, was next to the old smoke stack of the current central heating plant.

As is true today, murders in this area were relatively few and far between, so when they occurred, they made big news. The first hanging in St. Lawrence County happened in July 1816, as a result of a triple homicide on Route 37 in Louisville on February 22 of that year. The horrific murder took place at the home of Michael Scarborough and his family. A shady character named Gerteau lived next door and knew that Scarborough kept a large sum of money at his residence; he had seen the man holding a bundle of it the day before the murders. Gerteau formulated a plan to rob the house when he saw Scarborough leave for a business trip. Early the next morning, before anyone was awake, Gerteau slipped into the house, intending only to steal the money and run, but he noticed an axe inside the door and grabbed it, just in case. Mrs. Scarborough and her two children, as well as Gerteau's nephew who lived with the Scarboroughs as a hired hand, were all fast asleep. Gerteau snuck into Mrs. Scarborough's room, found the money—all $22 of it—and was about to flee when a wave of panic washed over him. For some reason known only to a killer's mind, he found himself raising the axe over Mrs. Scarborough's head and swinging a fatal blow that nearly decapitated the woman.

Like a wild dog with its first taste of blood, something snapped inside of him, and he proceeded through the house, killing the Scarborough's infant daughter and his own nephew the same way; he intended to kill the other Scarborough child, but unknowingly just wounded the young boy. Showing no remorse at all, the murderer feasted on treats he found in the home before fleeing the scene of the crime. With a full stomach, a pocketful full of money…and blood-saturated clothing, he made it just two miles before justice caught up with him. He had no choice but to confess, since he was covered in blood and had no wounds of his own to explain it. He was convicted of murder and hanged before a large crowd in Ogdensburg at the original county courthouse five months later.

The home where the murders took place still exists today, and some have told me that the owners must keep the light on upstairs at all times;

if they don't, they hear a young child crying and running about, apparently afraid of the dark.

* * *

The third person hanged for murder in the county was also an unsavory Louisville resident, although he seemed charming enough at first sight. James Eldridge, whose real name was later discovered to be Edwin Aldrich, was a handsome young man who moved to the area from the West to teach. Although not much was known about him, Eldridge was a very capable teacher and apparently a charming suitor, as well. Sarah Jane Gould was a beautiful Louisville widow who quickly fell for the suave out-of-towner. Before anyone knew it, the two were speaking of marriage. But early in 1857, Sarah became desperately ill. Prompt and proper medical treatment from her wise doctor hastened her recovery for a time, but then her fiancé insisted on taking charge of administering her medication. Nobody had any reason to question this request; but it wasn't long before Sarah's condition once again began to deteriorate, and she became gravely ill. She succumbed to her mysterious condition on May 26, 1857. Puzzled by the unexplainable turn of events, the physician ordered her remaining medication confiscated and tested. An investigation revealed that there were traces of arsenic in it. Sarah had been poisoned by her fiancé, the only person handling her medication. Eldridge was charged with murder and sentenced to be hanged in the county jail in Canton.

* * *

According to author Robert J. LaRue in his *St. Lawrence County Almanac* series, Peter Bresnaham was the last man hanged in St. Lawrence County. On April 30, 1878, Bresnaham, armed with two guns, went to a neighboring farm in South Colton with the intent of robbing Michael Daulter. Hiding across the road from Daulter's farm, he watched the man go about his business, and waited for his chance to kill, like a lion stalking its prey. That moment came when Daulter bent over to pick up something. The gunshot clipped him in the head but didn't kill him, so Daulter, bleeding profusely, attempted to flee to a neighbor's house. He never made it. Bresnaham grabbed Daulter's own axe and took off after the man. When he caught up with his victim, who by then had collapsed from shock in the middle of the road, he struck him in the head with the axe to finish him off, and then stole $1.25 and some tobacco from the dead man's pockets. Although the murderer attempted to disguise himself by shaving his beard, he had already been seen carrying the guns by several people who approached the scene of the crime.

Before he was hanged outside the jail in Canton, he confessed that he was a serial killer who had murdered a number of a Canadians before settling in St. Lawrence County.

Skull & Bones Society

Deer Island—Thousand Islands

Deer Island is such a benevolent name for an island owned and occasionally occupied by a secret society like the Skull & Bones. The forty-acre island, in the American channel two miles north of Alexandria Bay, was deeded to The Russell Trust Association (aka Skull & Bones Society) in 1927 by George Douglas Miller, who inherited the island from his father, Samuel Miller. The elder Miller purchased Deer Island in 1856 for $175. (It should be noted that the Miller family is one of the fifteen core family names embedded in the secret society since its inception in 1832.) At the time it was first deeded to Skull & Bones, the island had two houses, two tennis courts, softball fields, a bungalow, an amphitheater, and a boathouse. The Outlook, a fifteen-room structure built of stone and wood, contained volumes of rare books and antiques; but the contents and the building itself were lost to fire in 1949. Several of the original structures either lie in ruins or no longer exist; and it appears (at least to outsiders) that only one cottage remains in tact.

Deer Island was intended for use solely by Skull & Bones members and their families, as an island retreat—the Deer Island Club—where they could get together with old friends, host reunions, and hold annual meetings. According to the Deer Island Club articles of association, the purpose of the Club was to "promote the social intercourse of its members, and to provide for them facilities for recreation and social enjoyment; and to this end, to purchase, hold and convey any property, real or personal, which may be necessary or convenient therefore; to maintain a Club House for the use and benefit of its members; and to adopt by-laws and generally to exercise all the usual powers of corporations not prohibited by said statutes…"

The beautiful island, once brimming with gooseberry bushes and rhubarb plants, remains densely populated with White Pine, Hemlock, Oak, and Sugar Maple trees. It is still available exclusively to Skull & Bones members—and all new members pay at least one token visit—but it is strictly forbidden to the public at large, as it has been since the elite and enigmatic order acquired it. So, what exactly is the Order of Skull & Bones? Ahhh…that's a question even the top leaders of our country have a hard time answering—mainly because they're sworn to secrecy.

The society was founded in 1832 by William Huntington Russell and Alphonso Taft, two students who were disenchanted by Phi Beta Kappa at Yale University in New Haven, Connecticut. They started their own society, fashioning it after a secret German freemasonry society that Russell was introduced to in Europe the summer before his senior year at Yale. He befriended a leader of that society, had become privy to its bizarre clandestine rituals, and was encouraged to start up a similar society here in the States. That is why so many of the known practices and initiation rites of The Order, as it is called among initiates, have German and Nazi connotations (i.e. sitting in a tomb, lying in a coffin, eating from Hitler's silverware, the "skull and bones" symbols as worn by Nazi death camp guards, etc.).

The society inducts (or taps) exactly fifteen incoming seniors each year—generally those who exhibit potential or visible excellence in some area, or those who have familial ties with the society from the past. To refuse the invitation would be akin to refusing a certain life of power, fame, and wealth, because Skull & Bones Society members have each others' backs long after graduation from Yale, and most go on to live very prominent lives, thanks to the encouragement and behind-the-scenes support of their Skull brethren. The society is considered one of the most elite and powerful alumni networks in the country. Although it has managed to incorporate itself as a charitable organization that was allegedly worth over $4 million in 1999, it has been exempt from filing corporate reports with the State of Connecticut since 1943; thus, avoiding taxes and an accounting of its charitable contributions.

Although all members are sworn to everlasting secrecy regarding matters of The Order, some information has been disseminated by former Bonesmen who broke their vows and spoke on condition of anonymity, and some reporters and self-appointed tomb-raiders have acquired information not privy to the general public. Apparently, the process of inducting new initiates is somewhat alarming, considering the caliber of the inductees and the positions that they hold today. Sources say that initiates are required to bend over and kiss a skull, have a femur bone pressed against their backside, reenact a throat-slashing scene, and lie nude in a coffin—which symbolizes that they are to pass from the "barbarian world" and be reborn in "The Order." Finally, they pledge allegiance to a figure representing Satan and are endowed with a secret code name that they will forever be known as by fellow Bonesmen.

Some names are traditional and chosen based on the function of the individual; some are taken from mythology, religion, and literature; and some are passed on by their predecessors to specific beneficiaries each year, depending on certain character or physical traits. For example, the tallest member is always dubbed "Long Devil"; the member with the most sexual experience—something each individual is required to divulge to all other members in detail as part of their bonding—is always called Magog; the member with the least sexual experience is called Gog; and the varsity football team captain is always called Boaz.

You may be wondering what the President and Senator Kerry were called. Not surprisingly, Kerry was dubbed "Long Devil." The President's father, former President George H.W. Bush, *surprisingly*, was Magog; and the current President George W. Bush—generally considered a "legacy tap"—was just called "Temporary." Not for any prophetic reason; it's just that when he was invited to choose his own secret name (after learning that he wasn't the tallest, or the most experienced, or the least experienced, or the most athletic, literary, or mythical...), he couldn't come up with anything off the top of his head. So they put him out of his misery and called him "Temporary," which ironically became his permanent secret code name. Seriously.

I was unable to find what the President's grandfather Prescott Bush was called, but he was a legend in the Skull and Bones Society. It was he and a couple of other Bonesmen who allegedly stole the skull of Geronimo (the Apache chief) and delivered it to the Tomb (Bones clubhouse), where it remains today, along with a number of other skulls and bones.

Once inducted into the Skull and Bones Society, the lucky fifteen meet once or twice a week for their entire senior year inside a tomb at 64 High Street on Yale's campus. The primary purpose of the meetings is to bond with one another and provide mutual support that carries over into the rest of their lives. There, the up-and-coming movers and shakers of the world feast on gourmet meals served on Hitler's china and silverware and prepared by their own private chef. They are required to take turns lying in the coffin and revealing their sexual experiences, down to the minutest detail, from their earliest memory to their latest conquest. The clocks inside of the tomb are intentionally set five minutes ahead of the rest of the world so the Bonesmen feel separate and more "ahead" of the rest of the world.

Regardless of whether the information gathered to date about the secret society's rituals and covert activities is true or not, whatever goes on behind closed doors in the Tomb at Yale can't be all bad. Since the first day in 1832 that they began "tapping" upcoming seniors from Yale for initiation into their elite organization, Skull and Bones has somehow managed to tap into some of the most influential people walking among us.

So, if you happen to pass by Deer Island on a tour boat or speedboat and see someone walking on the shoreline, it's probably a V.I.P., or a new initiate well on his way to certain success.

Tricks...or Treats?

Parishville, Potsdam

St. Lawrence County was teaming with pranksters in the 1800s, and it didn't have to be April Fool's Day or Halloween to trick your neighbors; although, on one memorable occasion in town, it was the latter. On October 31, 1868, the Parishville Town Constable was in hot pursuit (on foot) of a young man who led him on a wild goose chase through the back streets of Parishville (not that there were many back then). The chase ended at the edge of a precipice where a footbridge had once existed—the last time the young man had seen it. As he approached the precipice, realizing that he had no other way out, the young man picked up speed and chanced an incredible leap across the twenty-six-foot-wide span. He made it, but just barely. He grabbed onto a bush hanging over the side of the embankment and pulled himself up to safety...and freedom.

The constable, who was aware that there was no longer a bridge there, was certain he would find the young man waiting dejectedly for him at the edge of the river. Imagine his surprise when he finally caught up and saw that his perpetrator had leapt to the other side. The constable, both shocked and impressed, conceded defeat diplomatically and then offered to buy the man a drink back at the hotel, adding, "The treat's on me." (So was the trick, I'd say.)

* * *

Potsdam had its share of tricksters, as well. One day in the 1800s, a Potsdam resident found a large egg and, using melted tallow, wrote "Woe, woe to those who deny the Trinity" on it. Then, by dipping the egg into vinegar, the shell disintegrated, leaving only the waxy portions where he had written. Pleased with his creation, the man placed the egg on the floor in the middle of the barn next door and waited. Sure enough, the egg was quickly found the next morning by a young lad, and it was laying right next to a hen. It didn't take long for word of the discovery to spread. Gullible as they were about such things in those days, the Trinitarians were delighted, of course. But the Unitarians were fearful that the world was coming to an end.

The prankster must have thought himself quite clever, tricking an entire township, but he took it a little too far. In his arrogance, he set out more and more inscribed eggs, until finally someone realized it was a hoax. The deceptive method of creating such eggs was uncovered, and all the hoopla quickly died down.

* * *

Another much crueler practical joke also took place in the early 1800s in Potsdam. A mischevious watchmaker dared a customer to drink acid from a dish that was used in the watch-making process, just for kicks. If the customer agreed, he would be given a free watch. But the customer was a little cleverer than the watchmaker. He agreed, and somehow faked swallowing the acidic liquid, so the watchmaker gave him his watch, and the customer went on his merry way, eager to tell the guys what had just transpired. Apparently, it must have happened on a Sunday, because none of the guys were working, and they had way too much time on their hands—time to come up with a devious plan for a practical joke. Keeping straight faces, several of the man's buddies went to the shop and confronted the watchmaker with tragic news. The man who drank the acid in his shop, they said, was now gravely ill, and they were there to help the man save himself from being hanged for murder. They recommended that he challenge the sick man to a duel; after all, he would surely win a battle with such a seriously ill man; and if he won, the only witness to the crime would be dead, and the watchmaker's secret would be safe.

So the patron and the watchmaker agreed to meet—each accompanied by a "second," which is the person in charge of loading their pistols. But the seconds had been instructed to only load powder into the guns and to not let the watchmaker know. Two shots rang out, and neither man had fallen. Tension was high by the time the men fired for a third time. On the third shot, the watchmaker went down with a thud. He felt the impact that knocked him over and suddenly realized what it must feel like to be fatally shot. Crying, he gave hasty instructions on how to dispose of his belongings and bid them all a heartfelt farewell. It must have pained him to see them all laughing and grinning as he lay there dying. Finally, when the laughter had subsided, someone explained to the poor watchmaker what had happened. They had played a cruel trick on him. The man he fed acid to wasn't dying. He was alive and well. And the watchmaker wasn't dying either. He had been punched by his second as part of the prank. *Punched.* His second had smacked him at the same moment shots were fired, making him think he'd been shot. The customer had gotten the last laugh—and still had that watch to show for it—but the watchmaker was so happy to find out that he wasn't dying that he offered to buy a gallon of rum for everyone.

The First Church

Massena

You think it's tough getting up to go to church *these days*? In 1819, Massena's very first church was built overlooking the Grasse River. It was a group effort of the Congregationalists, the Baptists, and the Adventists. The church was poorly heated, having only two woodstoves for heat, which was hardly enough to warm the parishioners, so they brought their own foot warmers—pierced tin boxes with hot charcoal inside, according to Eleanor Dumas, Massena town historian and author of *History of Massena, the Orphan Town*. Parishioners also brought their own hardwood "Bible boxes," which held their own family Bibles and served a dual purpose as foot stools—again, to keep the cold floor from freezing their feet.

Town roads of that time were few and far between, and they were bad enough to traverse in the summer, let alone in the winter when they were hidden under several feet of unplowed snow. There were no markers along the sides of the road to indicate to a God-fearing family on a horse and buggy that they were "on the right path." Then, after all of that rigmarole, they had to sit in a freezing church and try to warm their near-frozen feet with a couple of silly tin cans and, at the same time, try to concentrate on the sermon.

If that wasn't bad enough, the first church in Massena had a very strict code of behavior. If its rules were broken or parishioners sinned, they faced disciplinary action from the entire congregation. Their sins, both minor and mortal, were publicly confessed and reviewed by all. It was the congregation who chose the punishment or penance needed to save a member's soul.

So the next time you complain about having to get up and go to church, keep in mind how much better you have it than your predecessors in 1819.

Infamous Incidents

Earthquake!

Northern New York

As most northern New Yorkers know, we live smack in the middle of the Northern New York-Western Quebec Seismic Zone (also known as the Charlevoix-Kamouraska Zone) which is the most active earthquake zone in New York State, and the third most active earthquake zone on the entire East Coast. As such, we're somewhat accustomed to the occasional minor earthquake, but will "the big one" ever hit here in our lifetime? There is evidence that the earth's crust in this region is under stress, and it's believed by the scientific community that such stress is related to tectonic plate motions—the instigator of seismic activity in upwards of ninety-five percent of earthquakes—but, strangely, New York is far from any plate margins, so our earthquake activity is not well understood as of yet.

What is known, however, is that, since at least the seventeenth century, several hundred earthquakes with a magnitude greater than 2.0 and a handful of earthquakes in the 4-to-6.0 range on the Richter Scale have plagued this zone, which extends from the Adirondack Mountains to Western Quebec. The first recorded earthquake in the St. Lawrence Seaway River Valley occurred in 1663 and was so powerful—more than a 6.0 on today's Richter Scale—that the St. Lawrence River was muddied for some time with debris and clay, making it unsuitable for consumption. According to one account by a Jesuit priest who documented the Mohawks, the only people living in the region at that time, "The first shock was the most violent and commenced with a noise resembling thunder. The shock lasted half an hour. The earthquake continued almost without intermission." He said the violence of the earthquake was most apparent in the woods, "where it appeared as if there was a battle raging between the trees," as the earth heaved and palpated.

In 1832, an earthquake struck St. Lawrence County and was felt as far away as Montreal at 11:30 P.M. on January 22. Evert's *History of St. Lawrence County, N.Y.* described it thusly:

"...the tremulous motion of stoves, crockery and windows, with a sound like distant thunder beneath the surface of the earth, was distinctly perceived by those who had not yet retired to sleep." Some likened the oddity to the sound of "several heavy carriages passing rapidly over frozen ground." In 1867, an earthquake awakened residents from St. Lawrence County to Syracuse and Burlington, Vermont, and ten years later, an earthquake along the St. Lawrence River and Lake Champlain downed chimneys, cracked ceilings, and damaged windowpanes. Other strong earthquakes in the region followed, about every ten to twenty years: 1897, 1914, 1928, and 1934. Then on September 4, 1944, a 5.9 magnitude quake struck the Massena-Cornwall region, purportedly damaging or destroying ninety percent of the chimneys in Massena and Cornwall and damaging foundations, plumbing, wells, and masonry, causing an estimated $2 million worth of damage to both cities. Older residents recall cracks in the earth in nearby Hogansburg and heavy damage to brick and concrete structures in Malone, Norfolk, Ogdensburg, Waddington, Fort Covington, Massena, and Cornwall. The "Goodnow Earthquake" of 1983 was a 5.2 magnitude quake that caused damage in the central Adirondacks; especially in the Blue Mountain Lake area of Hamilton County. It caused tombstones to slide or rotate, plaster walls to crack, and damagd chimneys. Several landslides were reported and the quake was felt in twelve states and in two Canadian provinces.

The most recent damaging quake occurred in Au Sable Forks, a hamlet in the Town of Jay in Essex County, New York, in 2002. It measured 5.3 on the Richter Scale and primarily affected Essex and Clinton Counties. In a press release issued on May 9, 2002, by the governor's office, Governor George Pataki said, "While we fortunately avoided the loss of life and injuries, the Au Sable Forks earthquake of April 20 caused widespread suffering and tremendous financial hardship among our friends and neighbors in the North Country. As state agencies continue to do all that we can to help, federal assistance is needed to alleviate the severe suffering individuals experienced as a result of the quake." Nine hundred homes and businesses had foundation, chimney, or structural damage, as well as damage to their interior and exterior finishes. Churches, public buildings, and infrastructure such as dams, roads, culverts, and bridges were also reported damaged and compensation in federal disaster relief aid was sought. Public drinking water supplies were compromised, and at least three dams suffered damage requiring water levels to be lowered. Videos aired on local news channels, showing large gaps in pavement where roadways had collapsed or been washed out.

As I said, the pattern seems to be a damaging earthquake every ten to twenty years in this area. Although, sometimes it's only a few years in between, and sometimes it's thirty or forty. When or where the next earthquake strikes in the Northern New York-Western Quebec seismic zone is anyone's guess. But, just in case you were wondering, it's only about $60 a year to add earthquake coverage it to your current home-owners' fire insurance policy. I checked after writing this story!

The Horseman Cometh'

Ausable Chasm

Ausable Chasm, the "Grand Canyon of the East," was first opened as a tourist attraction in 1870, but the chasm itself was created some 15,000 years ago during the most recent Ice Age when it was carved out of 500-million-year-old rock. I don't know which is taller, the tales long associated with the chasm's history or the 125-foot-high walls that bore witness to the alleged exploits over the millennia.

One such tale from the *Plattsburgh Sentinel* (1897) was originally told by John Hilliard of the *Chicago Times-Herald*. The piece was called, "A Legend of the Au Sable: A Horseman Drove Across the Ghost of a Bridge." According to the article, an old man named Max Morgan rode into town one night on his horse, and since he had lived nearby years earlier and had helped to build the chasm's old wooden bridge known as the High Bridge in 1793, he had no problem finding and crossing the chasm with his horse on that starless night. At least that's what the weary and hungry stranger told the owner of a tavern adjacent to the chasm, when the inn-keeper asked him if he had any trouble finding his way over. But the tavern owner just stared at the man, as if both amused and insulted.

After a hushed silence, all present proceeded to tell the man that the bridge he spoke of—the old wooden bridge made of Norway Pine logs—had been washed away long before; and, by 1810 or so, all that remained was a single, narrow "stringer" (or log) spanning the chasm from one side to the other. Surely the man and his horse could not have crossed such a precarious structure without falling to their deaths on a night as pitch black as that. But the man insisted that, although he could see nothing, he heard his horse's hooves trotting across the planking and was certain they were crossing the chasm, because he heard the familiar sound of the water below. With neither man backing down, a bet was waged as to the existence of the bridge.

The next morning, practically all of the townspeople met at the site of the old bridge. The storyteller said, "Sure enough, in the soft sand of the road, there were footprints of a horse, and the trail led from the stringer across the chasm up to the tavern porch. One young daredevil walked across the narrow stringer and made a startling discovery. There was a similar trail on the other side." So it was true! The man had unknowingly ridden his horse in complete and utter darkness across the deep and deadly chasm on nothing more than a log, believing it to be the original wooden bridge he had helped to construct. Shocked and horrified at the realization, the man began trembling so violently that "the shakes" remained with him for the rest of his life; and, in the blink of an eye, it is said that the man's hair changed from black to white. But he wasn't the only person to meet a nearly-disastrous or tragic fate at Ausable Chasm.

According to the local attraction's website, one man, while delivering a load of stones to the ledge near the present entrance to the chasm, fell into the raging river below—load and all—when the ledge collapsed from the weight. Incredibly, the man was only slightly injured.

The Reverend John Dyer was not as fortunate when he plunged to his death in 1870. At that time, only a large log which had been flattened on top for easier walking connected Table Rock to the other side of the chasm. Before realizing how slippery the log had become on that humid summer day, the young minister stepped onto the log while at the same time reaching for his girlfriend's hand. Right before her eyes, he slipped and plunged to the water many feet below, quickly being lost to the turbulence. Some sources end that tale with the minister's girlfriend remaining at the chasm until she wasted away to nothing and died of a broken heart.

Lady in the Lake

Lake Placid

"You probably don't even know who I am, or what I look like..."
—A former student wrote those poignant words in a note to Mabel Smith Douglass in 1933. Thirty years later, Smith Douglass's remains seemed to whisper the same...

Prior to 1963, an apparition of a woman was seen several times near Pulpit Rock in Lake Placid. In September of that year, two divers exploring the bottom of the lake at that very location discovered what they at first believed was a discarded store mannequin. They quickly realized it was a human body. The water temperature where the body was found 105 feet below the surface was a frigid thirty-four degrees. Combined with the high calcium salt chemical composition of the water, it was a recipe for "adipocere," a physiological reaction in which chemical minerals and salts replace body tissue, forming a somewhat effective barrier against total decomposition of a submerged cadaver. The result is a waxy shell of the individual who inhabited the body.

According to reporter Barney Fowler, the scuba divers said the body was found lying on its right side "in a deposit of silt" with a rope knotted around the neck. On closer examination, the divers found that the other end of the rope was attached to an old-fashioned anchor. The rope disintegrated unexpectedly when the divers touched it; and the body, naked but for an unusual pair of shoes and a thin strip of elastic around one thigh, detached from its rope and anchor and began to float up, while the anchor settled deeper into the silt. Having no choice, the divers gently guided their gruesome and fragile discovery to the surface, where

Mabel Smith Douglass.
Old newspaper photograph dated 1922.

they temporarily affixed it to a buoy while they prepared to bring it on board their boat. Tragically, in that short amount of time, several speed boats went by, causing large waves to jostle the buoy. The jarring of the remains caused the corpse to fall apart—the head, neck (with attached rope), as well as the left arm and right hand all broke off and sank back to their murky grave. Another diver was quickly sent to retrieve what he could, but the remains plunged into the silt—making it difficult to find them. All he was able to recover, after a long and arduous search, was the head. But it was in far worse condition than when the body was originally discovered. For thirty years, the corpse had lain on the placid lake bottom undisturbed, where it remained remarkably well-preserved, except for the partial ossification. When it was first found, the facial features were still recognizable; but the trauma suffered by the fragile remains in its short journey to the surface caused the facial features to erode and vanish—as if someone had wiped them off the head. Worse, the jawbone had become dislodged in the recovery of the head from the silt, so there were no longer jaws teeth to help identify the victim. At least, not right then.

Soon, state troopers and the local coroner had arrived at the scene.

Early in the course of their investigation, they were tipped off by a Lake Placid tour boat operator that their dead woman might be the famous Mabel Smith Douglass (born Anna Mabel Smith), who disappeared in that general vicinity in 1933. While they were pursuing that lead, an autopsy was being performed on the remains. The autopsy revealed that it was indeed the body of a Caucasian woman who had been approximately 5'5" tall and weighed 140 pounds. She had given birth at least once, and there was no sign of external injuries to what remained of the atrophying tissue—in other words, there didn't appear to have been foul play involved in her death. As stated earlier, all that remained of her clothing was a thin strip of elastic like that from an undergarment around the right thigh and a pair of shoes that a local shoe expert said had been worn by the wealthy in the thirties.

All of what the police investigation and autopsy revealed thus far, along with the fact that, besides Mrs. Douglass, no other females had reportedly drowned or gone missing in that area of the lake, quickly convinced officials they had found the long-lost woman, but the investigation continued with more and more evidence mounting daily. Mrs. Douglass, they learned, was the founder and first dean of the New Jersey College for Women (now known as Douglass College, the women's college of Rutgers University). The college opened in 1918, as a result of her dogged pursuit of funding for the institution and her determination that women of all economic classes deserved a higher education. But the woman who gave so much of herself—her time, her money, and her energy—to ensure the happiness of others had a life fraught with tragedy.

Born in Jersey City, in 1877, Anna Mabel Smith was a highly intelligent and giving child. She received her bachelor's degree in arts from Barnard College in 1899 and was one of the first graduates of that school—a sister school of Columbia University. Always a supporter of education, she taught elementary school in Manhattan until 1903 when she married William Douglass. The couple had two children—a son and a daughter. All was right with their world. Then, in 1911, Smith Douglass decided that the all-male Rutgers College should open a sister college for women. So dedicated to this cause was she, that she used her own money and the money she raised over the next five or six years to see the project through. By the time her dream was realized, and the

New Jersey College for Women opened, her husband and mother had both passed away. The Spanish flu reached the States the same year the college opened, and Smith Douglass helped nurse her students through that deadly virus. Five years later, her only son committed suicide. All she had left was her daughter. Smith Douglass's health began to deteriorate in the early 1930s. By 1932, she requested a leave of absence, to the concern of friends and colleagues. One woman later told police that it was well-known that Smith Douglass suffered a setback in the stock market around that same time. In May 1933, Smith Douglass resigned as dean and moved to her camp in Lake Placid, presumably to recuperate. But just four months after leaving the college—and all that she ever worked for—she vanished near Pulpit Rock, after being seen in a St. Lawrence skiff rowboat which was later found capsized. Her disappearance made headlines, and a massive search for her body was undertaken, but no body was ever found…until the two divers came upon it unwittingly almost exactly thirty years later.

Three days after the original discovery at the bottom of the lake, two different divers from Plattsburgh found the missing jawbone and some teeth. While the police were still unable to make a positive identification based on dental records (Smith Douglass' dentist had long since passed away, and his files had all been destroyed), they were able to discern from a dentist in Lake Placid that the teeth were gold inlays; and a friend of Mrs. Douglass' recalled that the deceased did, in fact, have inlays. Further, divers who first found the body reported to police that the anchor they had seen (before it was lost in the silt) was bell shaped. In researching police records from 1933, it was discovered that Mrs. Douglass' daughter told the police at that time that a bell-shaped anchor was missing from their boat house. Sadly, the police were unable to obtain more information from Smith Douglass' daughter, because she, too, died tragically in 1948, from a fall—an entire family wiped out by tragedy.

At any rate, there was more than enough evidence for the police to issue a statement regarding the unsolved disappearance of Smith Douglass in 1933 and the discovery of her well-preserved body in 1963. The death was ruled accidental, even though much evidence points to the possibility of suicide, and many people to this day believe that it was. The official police statement, issued by the Bureau of Criminal

Investigation in Saranac Lake said:

"State Police investigation into the recovery and identification of an unknown body from Lake Placid by members of the Lake Champlain Wreck Raiders Diving Club, has identified the body as Mabel Smith Douglass, who vanished September 21, 1933. The investigation reveals no evidence of a criminal homicide.

"The investigation does reflect ill health and an extreme nervous condition of Mrs. Douglass, but since positive factual evidence is lacking, and the rope the skin divers saw around the neck disintegrated when touched, examination of a knot or accidental entanglement in an anchor rope cannot be determined.

"Therefore, the official coroner's verdict is accidental death."

Smith Douglass' body was claimed by Douglass College and buried at Greenwood Cemetery in Brooklyn, beside her husband and children. Not only is she believed to have haunted Pulpit Rock in Lake Placid, but some students believe that either she or her children still haunt the Little Theater on the campus she founded where unexplained phenomena are known to occur. I hope that's not the case. Her legacy will live on, but her soul deserves the eternal rest it may have sought at the bottom of a lake called Placid.

Blood Libel

Massena

On the evening of September 22, 1928, a four-year-old girl named Barbara Griffith disappeared from her home in the Massena-Norfolk area. The events that transpired during the next twenty-four hours wreaked havoc on a family, a town, and, indeed, an entire nation. For it was here, in the heart of the North Country, that North America experienced its first case of blood libel—a term long used to accuse Jews of murdering non-Jewish children and using their blood to make matzoh for Passover.

In ancient and medieval times, it was not uncommon for Jews to be accused of ritual murder by Christians, because the Jewish celebration of Passover consisted of putting the blood of a lamb on one's doorpost to celebrate their escape from Egypt during biblical times. Over the years, there were libelous accusations that the blood of Christian children was used for this purpose, and as an ingredient in the celebratory bread of Passover, matzoh. In reality, the only ingredients in matzoh are flour and water which are baked into flat, unleavened bread to commemorate the unleavened bread eaten by the Jews when they fled Egypt so quickly that they didn't have time for their dough to rise.

Unfortunately, some of the non-Jewish residents of Massena in 1928 were not well-educated in the basics of Jewish custom, or the whole sorry affair might never have occurred. It began with a Greek immigrant named Albert Comnas suggesting to the state police that perhaps the child had been kidnapped by the Jews for ritual sacrifice, because it was, after all, he said, the evening before Yom Kippur—the most important

Jewish holiday of the year—and a non-Jewish child's blood was sup-posed to be used in food preparation, according to a legend he vaguely recalled. Yom Kippur is the Day of Atonement for Jews, and there is no special food prepared, because it's a day of fasting and atoning for sins of the previous year. In fact, at about the same time little Barbara first was reported missing, the state of fasting had already begun for Massena's Jewish community (the fast begins the evening before Yom Kippur at sunset and ends 25-hours later). Why would someone kidnap and slaugh-ter a child when they are in a state of atonement, and why would they need blood for food when they are fasting? Comnas was mistaking Yom Kippur for Passover, when matzoh is carefully prepared and eaten, and his ignorance and intolerance incited a riot in downtown Massena.

At one misguided individual's prompting, and apparently with Massena Mayor W. Gilbert Hawes' approval, State Trooper H.M. McCann called the respected Rabbi Berel Brennglass, of the Adath Israel synagogue in Massena, down to the police station where he was interrogated about Jewish customs and practices for more than an hour. The rabbi emphat-ically denied that Jews killed children in any of their rituals. According to *Time* magazine's October 15, 1928, edition, a mob of several hundred angry people waited outside the police headquarters for someone to blame the child's disappearance on, until it was reported that the little girl had been found wandering out of the forest between Norfolk and Massena after spending the night lost in the woods. She had wandered off into the forest looking for her brother. She was unharmed and obliv-ious to what had transpired as a result of her disappearance. And while it was certainly good news and a relief to her family and community, the ripple effect of the incident was fast spreading across the globe.

Even after Barbara Griffith was found unscathed and admitted to wandering off by herself, there were those, including the mayor, who believed the Jews had released the girl when they realized their plan was foiled, so the mayor ordered a boycott of Massena's Jewish-owned busi-nesses. Ku Klux Klan members blocked Massena's downtown streets and surrounded the synagogue, shouting obscenities and threats at Jewish residents. The Jewish community alerted Louis Marshall, President of the American Jewish Committee, and famed Rabbi Stephen Samuel Wise, Chairman of the American Jewish Congress. The situation was spinning rapidly out of control. Rabbi Wise complained to Major John A. Warner, New York State Police Superintendent, and to his friend, New York State Governor Al Smith about the treatment he received from Trooper McCann. Governor Smith assured Wise that McCann would be investigated. Major Warner soon reported to the Governor that McCann had been suspended after a severe reprimand.

As for Massena's Mayor Hawes, Marshall sent a scathing letter to him which said, in part:

"What has occurred does not merely affect the Jews of Massena, whose very lives were placed in jeopardy, but the entire Jewish population of this country and of the world...I deem it my duty to demand of you an immediate and public written apology to the Jewish people for the terrible wrong which you have inflicted upon them.

"This apology must be couched in such terms as will meet with my approval, so that the world may know that the remorse which you have expressed is genuine. As further evidence, you should also resign from the office which you now hold." (Hawes was actually reelected for a sixth consecutive term.)

Mayor Hawes quickly responded in kind to Marshall by accepting responsibility for his actions and showing remorse. He said:

"I clearly see and I have no hesitation in affirming that when first the suggestion was made that the disappearance of the Griffith child might be associated with the alleged practice of human sacrifice by the Jews, far from giving hospitable ear to the suggestion, I should have repelled it with indignation and advised the State trooper to desist from his intention of making inquiry of the respected rabbi of the Jewish community of Massena concerning a rumor so monstrous and fantastic. I do not make this statement of profound regret because of any fear on my part that charges will be brought against me looking to my removal from the office of Mayor to which I have been elected five times..."

The good Rabbi Brennglass, who bore the brunt of intolerance against Massena's Jews, offered words of wisdom and forgiveness at his evening Yom Kippur service, less than 24 hours after "The Incident at Massena," as it has come to be known, first began. He told his shaken congregation, "We must forever remind ourselves that this happened in America, not tsarist Russia, (but) among people we have come to regard as our friends. We must show our neighbors that their hatred originates in fear, and that this fear has its roots in ignorance. We must show them they have nothing to fear from us. We must tell the world this story so it will never happen again." It had to be difficult for the Jews to face their non-Jewish friends and neighbors after such an ordeal, but in time, Massena's townspeople pulled back together and carried on, knowing that not only had they learned from their mistakes that day, but the whole world had learned something about tolerance and humanity, as well.

Like the American Jewish Historical Society states on their website, a quiet city in upstate New York with a relatively small Jewish population that supports but one synagogue "seems an unlikely location for a major event in American Jewish history, but it was."

The Really, Truly Shortest Summer

Northern New York

We often complain up here about our short summers and long winters, but I don't remember ever seeing snow in June or a widespread, killing frost in July. Yet, that's exactly what our North Country predecessors experienced in 1816—the year there was no summer. And it wasn't just one rare summer day of snow or the occasional day of frost…it was winter-like weather practically every day of the summer, and it led to near-starvation and poverty for the majority of local residents.

The year started out with a dry winter and a dry, late spring. Not only was precipitation much lower than normal from March through May, but so was the temperature. Vegetation stalled. When the hay ran out, cattle had to be fed corn meant for human consumption. On May 28, a particularly strong cold front brought ice accumulation and a light dusting of snow to the area. Fruit trees and corn stalks struggled to remain viable. Then on June 6, a heavy and widespread snowstorm mixed with hail stunned area residents…and the destruction of crops became imminent. Elizabethtown in Essex County, for example, reported a three-hour snowstorm which killed most of that town's garden vegetables. Five to six more inches of steadily-falling snow followed the next day, and the day after that.

Not only were plants dying, but birds and sheep were freezing to death. Families were struggling to survive with no food and little warmth. the Danville (Connecticut) *North Star* from June 15, 1816, reported: "Some account was given in last week's issue of the unparalleled severity of the weather. It continued without any essential amelioration, from the 6th to the 10th, instant-freezing as hard five nights in succession as it usually does in December…Saturday morning the weather was more severe than it generally is during the storms of winter." Then a few blessed days of summer-like weather arrived at the end of June and into the first few days of July. But on July 6, hopes were shattered as another cold front plunged daytime temperatures back into the forties.

The diary of Artemus Kent of Hopkinton in St. Lawrence County had the following entry on July 11: "All crops are very backward and promise but little. Many of our neighbors are without bread." The remainder of July and all of August were plagued by weeks of frost, interlaced sporadically with several days at a time of more seasonal weather; just enough to get people's hopes up that the bizarre weather was over for good. Finally, in mid-September the unseasonable frosts caught up to the normal, seasonal weather, and the drought broke.

Thus, the summer of 1816 went down in history—not just in Northern New York, but in the entire Northeast—as the coldest summer in recorded history, based on 175 years of meteorological records. But what caused this meteorological event? The most popular theory is that a number of major volcanic eruptions in the four years preceding 1816 caused massive amounts of volcanic dust to be blown into the atmosphere where it accumulated and settled over the Northeast—and many other areas of the world—for one unforgettable year, causing drastic changes in atmospheric conditions of the affected regions. Another possibility is that the weather of 1816 was simply a result of an extraordinary sequence of weather events occurring at the right place and time to forge a season-long disruption in weather patterns.

Wacky Wilderness

Dino-Beings

Whitehall

I've heard about a lot of strange creatures besides ghosts in these parts. According to local residents, this region is teeming with unexplained beings, from hairy man-beasts to lake monsters and shadowpeople. I was foolish enough to think I'd actually heard it all, but, of course, I was wrong. Steve A. shared his very unique experience with me, after he read about other strange sightings in his hometown in my book, *Haunted New York: Ghosts and Strange Phenomena of the Empire State.*

It happened in the 1970s on his father's property in the town of Whitehall in the Adirondacks. Steve was about eleven and was walking along the stream at the back of the property when he spotted "two odd prehistoric-looking 'creatures'" standing upright on two legs in a couple inches of water near the shore. They were very small, only about six to eight inches tall, and were tumbling over each other as if at play. Steve clearly recalls that they were greenish-brown and looked to be half dinosaur and half man—certainly not like anything he had ever seen before or that he has seen since. He immediately thought to himself, "I thought those didn't exist anymore," because they looked more prehistoric than anything else that came to mind. He stared in awe for perhaps eight to ten seconds and then glanced away, but when he looked back, they were gone.

Thinking that his father would think he had just imagined it, he kept it to himself all these years. Steve had pet newts as a child, and he knows that the little creatures he saw that day were definitely not lizards, or any other identifiable species he's aware of, for that matter. He can think of nothing to explain what he saw. Mutant products of Adirondack acid rain?

The Big Buck

Paul Smith's

Courtesy of *Adirondack Album—Volume Two* by Barney Fowler

Photo of 42-point buck

Around 1900, a 42-point buck was killed near Paul Smith's in Franklin County? That's right...a record-breaking forty-two points. I'm telling you, it's got to be the early Adirondack acid rain!

According to Barney Fowler in *Adirondack Album—Volume Two*, the rare and impressive head and rack above graced the wall behind the front desk of a local hotel until a fire gutted the place, after which its whereabouts could not be traced. While Fowler was able to obtain a photo of the mounting before the fire, the actual location of the trophy head, if it still exists, is as mysterious as the identity of the lucky hunter who killed it in the first place.

Lake Monsters and Such

Waddington, Hermon, Norfolk

By far the most popular of our North Country lake monsters is Champ, the Lake Champlain monster. Champ has had more than its share of publicity and notoriety, but there have been sightings of many other unexplained large lake creatures all around Northern New York for centuries that also deserve fifteen minutes of fame.

Two highly respected brothers from Waddington promoted the existence of a St. Lawrence River creature with similarities to Champ in the '80s. But they weren't the first to report St. Lawrence "sea serpent" sightings. The early Native American inhabitants of St. Regis called the creature "the Manitou." In 1874, after sightings of the Manitou were reported again along the St. Lawrence River, three non-Native skeptics were dispatched to investigate, according to *The Manufacturer & Builder Magazine* (1874), and they claimed that what the Indians actually saw was nothing more sinister than debris such as logs bobbing up and down in the water as a result of gas that was rushing to the surface.

The three skeptics might have been quite smug with their little theory, but another sea monster sighting in the Gulf of St. Lawrence eighteen years later added credibility to the original sea-serpent theory. In that case, according to *The Century Magazine* (1892), "A sea-monster appeared at Maringomish, in the Gulf of St. Lawrence, judged to be a hundred feet in length. It was seen by two intelligent observers, nearly aground, in calm waters, within two hundred feet of the beach."

There was also a cluster of sea serpent sightings in the town of Hermon in the 1880s and 1890s according to author Robert J. LaRue.

Known as the "Trout Lake Sea Monster," LaRue said it was described by one witness, the local game protector, as "having the head of a lynx, with a body several inches in diameter and fins as large as an oar blade." A Gouverneur businessman relaxing on the lake that year also reported seeing a creature he said had the head of a dog with an extremely thick neck. He shot at it from his rowboat but missed. A Baptist minister from Canton described the creature the same as the businessman had. He, too, shot and missed. Besides the game protector, businessman, and minister, many local residents enjoying recreational activities on Trout Lake also spotted what they believed to be the "Trout Lake Sea Monster" for the next ten years, until the sightings finally ended in the late 1890s.

You may think it's improbable that so-called 'sea serpents' could find their way inland to our local lakes and rivers, but perhaps they did just that more than ten thousand years ago when the Champlain Sea covered much of Northern New York, just before the most recent Ice Age, and they've somehow adapted to their new surroundings over the course of several millennia. Maybe our local sea serpents and lake creatures are the very same legendary monsters witnessed for centuries off the coast of Massachusetts by colonial seafarers; and maybe that's why the physical characteristics of these mysterious, ever-elusive creatures often sound so prehistoric.

Speaking of sea creatures, did you know that a prehistoric Beluga whale was discovered in the St. Lawrence County town of Norfolk in 1987? Fifty-seven bones and bone fragments were unearthed at a construction site in clay just ten feet below the surface. Radiocarbon dating showed the remains to be approximately 10,450 years old and the whale was estimated to have been twelve feet long, based on a partial reconstruction of the skeleton. The whale is yet another reminder of the Ice Age and the Champlain Sea that once existed here in Northern New York.

Who's Afraid of the Big Bad Wolf?

Adirondacks

Canis lupus lycaon...it's the scientific name for the Eastern Timber Wolf, which roamed the Adirondacks and outlying areas freely in the 1800s...perhaps a tad too freely, according to the majority of people during that time period.

In the late eighteen hundreds, believe it or not, there were thought to be so many wolves and panthers (Felis concolor) in the North Country counties of Essex, Franklin, Hamilton, Herkimer, Lewis, and St. Lawrence that the State of New York implemented a bounty system in which any person who killed those species was paid between twenty and thirty dollars per carcass. There was a growing hysteria that wolves and panthers (also referred to as cougar, puma, catamount, and mountain lion) would otherwise kill off the livestock of North Country residents—and back then, a man's livestock was essential to provide sustenance for his family through the harsh Adirondack winters. In actuality, the wolf's primary prey typically consists of deer, moose, and beavers— and generally only the weakest and oldest of those. But with the publication of the wildly-popular version of *Little Red Riding Hood* written by the Brothers Grimm in 1857 and Jacob Halliwell's *The Story of the Three Little Pigs* (1849), a growing epidemic of fear caused the wolf to become stigmatized as a killing machine.

"Who's afraid of the big bad wolf?" In the nineteenth century, everyone living in the back woods of Northern New York was! So the bounty hunt began, in 1871, under New York State law. At twenty to thirty bucks a pop, it was not hard to find enough eager and able bounty hunters in these parts, but none could compare to George Muir, a slight man who wore his age well and avoided contact with others—like many Adirondack hermits of his day. The legendary Muir was known as the greatest wolf and panther hunter of the Adirondacks of that time period. According to reporter Barney Fowler, of the ninety-eight wolves killed during the twenty-year bounty hunt, Muir killed thirty-nine; and he took more than half of the hundred and seven panthers killed. According to a table of bounties paid in New York under the law of 1871, the vast majority of Muir's kills were made in St. Lawrence, Lewis, Herkimer, and Hamilton Counties. Most of his panthers were killed in the Towns of Long Lake, Wilmurt, Diana, Fine, and Pitcairn; and most of his wolves were killed in the Towns of Diana, Clifton, Fine, and Pitcairn. The peak years for total bounties paid for carcasses brought in were 1882 and 1883. After that, the numbers dropped drastically and rapidly, until by 1899 very few wolves and panthers remained in the Adirondacks, except in the most remote, wildest regions.

As for George Muir, he died at the age of eighty, doing exactly what he would have chosen to be doing at the time of his death. He was found lying on the ground in the woods, with his snowshoes leaning against a tree nearby, and his faithful dog guarding its deceased master until a familiar face arrived to claim the body. About the same time Muir died, a wolf rescuer named Aldo Leopold—known as the father of modern wildlife management—began efforts to preserve not only wolves in the wilderness, but all wildlife. In 1973, the Endangered Species Act was passed, and wolf conservation and management as we know it today was born. Due to the protection and mandates written into that act, wolves are being slowly and diligently restored to their original habitats in many parts of the country, with much success in the West and upper Midwest—and wolves have been upgraded from the endangered category to the "threatened" category. But wolf restoration in the Adirondacks is a hotly debated topic and not one that will soon be settled. Advocates believe wolves would be good for the Adirondack ecosystem—helping to control the deer population and benefiting many plant species and, thereby, smaller animals. But others, including the State, believe wolves might not be compatible with the best interests of farmers and residents in their habitat.

It is generally believed by state and federal wildlife officials that no more wolves exist in Northern New York, and that the Eastern Timber Wolf which once roamed freely here can now be found only in Minnesota, Wisconsin, and Michigan. However, several wolf-like animals killed in Vermont, Maine, and the bordering Quebec region since 1993 have been confirmed by laboratory analysis as being purebred and hybrid wolves, and, according to the *Sunday Leader-Herald* dated May 23, 2004, an Edinburgh man shot the first confirmed Adirondack wolf in a century, thinking it was a larger-than-average coyote. This fact was confirmed by the U.S. Fish and Wildlife Service through genetic analysis. Luckily for the man, he wasn't fined the permissible $100,000 fine for killing a wolf, since he had been told by DEC officials that wolves no longer exist in this area!

So the next time a North Country neighbor tells you they think they've seen a wolf...or a panther, for that matter, don't be too shocked. Both have been reported in local newspapers sporadically in the past decades as still running wild in the Adirondacks.

Peculiar People

Chippewa Bay's Hermits

Hammond

The North Country had its hermits even beyond the Adirondack Park boundaries. Chippewa Bay near Hammond was home to at least two. One was Hammond's first resident, William O'Neill, who lived in a cave for several years until the first settlers arrived in 1812. And, although, he chose to live in a cave, O'Neill wasn't nearly as unusual as Ezra Brockway. Brockway lived just off the shoreline of Hammond on an island in Chippewa Bay—an island he refused to pay taxes on, because he claimed it belonged to him! Even if they had wanted to, nobody could argue. After all, they felt sorry for the poor old coot. According to the hermit, his mother had been murdered in Ogdensburg, and he was sent out alone in a boat on the St. Lawrence River as a very young child. The boat drifted to the Canadian side where a kind-hearted man found him and raised him as his own son. Many believed the hermit was insane—and those suspicions were only heightened when Brockway began claiming that he was the son of Napoleon Bonaparte and that he was told so in a vision.

According to author Robert J. LaRue, Brockway's half-frozen body was discovered by a group of people crossing the ice on the St. Lawrence in February 1876. They saw that his cabin doors were open, and as they approached, they noticed snow drifting inside of the cabin. Inside they found Brockway on the verge of death. He told them that he had another vision—this one telling him to stop heating his home. He died a few days later from complications of hypothermia, and his body was buried in the old schoolhouse cemetery in Hammond.

Cold River City, Population 1

Adirondacks

Noah John Rondeau is a household name in the Adirondacks. He achieved celebrity despite his secluded lifestyle. But the size of the slight man with the modest ego belied his fame. Rondeau was born in 1883—the first of nine children born to a poor French-Canadian couple. His parents emigrated from Canada to the Au Sable Forks area where they raised Rondeau and his siblings on a small farm. Noah's parents wanted what was best for all their children, but Noah was headstrong and lacked the interest to buckle down. School was difficult for him and he quit. It wasn't until years later, when Rondeau was 26 years old, that he returned to school for a short period of time and earned an 8th grade diploma.

As a teenager, he tried his hand at various trades. Besides his well-publicized skills as a barber, which wouldn't do him much good in the wild, he gained valuable skills in carpentry, painting, and masonry. Also contributing to Noah's level of woodcraft was Daniel Emmett, an Abenaki Indian whom Noah met on the Raquette River.

Rondeau began to spend more and more time in the remote Cold River area and less time in civilized society. In 1929, at the age of forty-six, Rondeau set up permanent residence at Cold River. He became known as the Mayor of Cold River City, population: one. He built himself a Town Hall and a Hall of Records, as well as several teepee-like structures made of cut logs that he would tear apart through the winter to use as firewood. But the teepees served as his sleeping and living quarters during the warm months, and he built new ones year after year. The Town Hall, which now stands in all its original glory at the

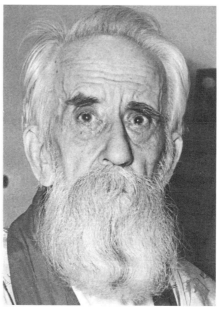

Courtesy of *Adirondack Album—Volume Two* by Barney Fowler

Last photograph of Noah John Rondeau

Adirondack Museum at Blue Mountain Lake, was nothing more than a makeshift cabin, eight by ten feet in size and low in height. It was covered by canvas and tar paper which was held in place with rocks, nails, and poles. In the cold winter months, the Town Hall was Rondeau's lodging place, and he kept it warm with a fifty-five-gallon drum he rigged as a crude yet efficient stove.

The Hall of Records was constructed in the same manner as the Town Hall, but it served as his library and guest quarters. It contained at least sixty books on topics such as astronomy, philosophy, history, science, and religion. He was an avid reader and kept many journals. Much of his writing was written in a code that Rondeau formulated himself.

Rondeau's few other notable possessions included his pipe, his rocker, and his violin, which he taught himself to play. He took it out whenever he had company to play for, which became more frequent as he gained notoriety. People who heard Noah's playing say it was a one-of-a-kind sound. Noah said the sound was amusingly entertaining back in the woods.

Rondeau hosted many hikers who traveled the Northville-Placid Trail which ran close to his "city." The most famous were probably

Grace Hudowalski and Dr. Orra Phelps—both Adirondack legends in their own right. Hudowalski was the first woman to scale all forty-six of the Adirondack High Peaks. Speaking ever fondly of her friend, she said Noah wore buckskin trousers and a buckskin vest, both finely stitched. The bag he wore slung over his shoulder was "made of un-seamed deer neck." She said he had a "kindly face," a black beard, and a twinkle in his brown eyes. He was a handsome man who was kind, gracious, and jovial, with a good sense of humor, according to those who knew him well.

All of his wonderful traits and the fact that he lived such an interesting, self-sustaining life alone in the wild made him appealing to the masses. Rondeau became something of a DEC poster child, in effect, after an article about him appeared in the *New York Conservationist* in 1946. In early 1947, the New York State Department of Environmental Conservation (DEC) flew him by helicopter out of the woods and then transported him to New York City for the National Sportsmen's Show, where he was a huge hit with the people. Noah was living proof of New York State's diversity—a state where you can live in the country's most populated city or a few hours north, alone in the primitive wilderness. One metropolitan journalist said Rondeau was such an important figure because he practiced what he preached—taking out of the wild only what he needed to survive, and replacing, as best as he could, what he took.

With his newfound fame, Rondeau attended sportsmen's shows and public engagements—a far cry from life as a hermit. A devastating wind called "The Big Blow" tore through the Adirondacks in 1950, causing such massive damage to the state forests that the DEC had to close much of the Adirondacks to the public for three years. It was the end of Cold River City, for Rondeau never returned "home" after that. He continued traveling to an occasional show, talking about what it was like to live in the woods. Noah even worked briefly at the North Pole in Wilmington as none other than Santa himself. He then lived on Social Security and stayed with various friends and relatives, and at boarding houses, for the next 15 years. During that time period, he stayed in Lake Placid, Saranac Lake, and Wilmington. Although Noah was no longer able to live in the wilderness, he harbored many fine memories of the old times.

By the summer of 1967, Rondeau's health had deteriorated to the point of requiring hospitalization, and on August 24 of that year, the eighty-three-year-old hermit passed away at Placid Memorial Hospital. Though he had requested he be buried at his hermitage, Essex County buried him at North Elba Cemetery. If you get a chance to visit his gravesite, be sure to leave some wild daisies, just like the ones he used to plant around his cabin in Cold River City.

The Oldest Person in the World

Stark

Courtesy of *Adirondack Album—Volume Two* by Barney Fowler

Photo of famous portrait of Delina Filkins

Before censuses were ever taken and historical records were scarce, anyone could claim to be the oldest person in the world and enjoy their moment of fame in their respective community. Nobody has ever topped Methuselah—the Book of Genesis's biblical patriarch who lived to be an alleged 969 years old—but, then again, nobody has ever been able to substantiate his claim either. Be that as it may, in modern times it's rare to hear of anyone reaching that status of supercentenarian—110 years old or older. In fact, the oldest recorded, historically-validated supercentenarian to date, France native Jeanne Calment, died in 1997 at 122 years of age. But there was someone closer to home who was the first person ever to officially reach 113 years of age—Herkimer County's Delina "Grandma" Filkins. And for a time, she was officially the Oldest Person in the World.

Delina (Ecker) Filkins was born in the Town of Stark on May 4, 1815, and spent her entire life living within a ten-mile radius of her childhood home. The only time she ever moved out of Herkimer County was when she moved in with her grandson for the last two months of her life; and—even more remarkably—the only time she was ever bedridden was for the last three days of her life.

Delina Ecker dropped out of school at age eleven to work at home spinning flax for yarn. At nineteen, she married a neighborhood man— one of many early suitors—John Filkins. The newlyweds moved into John's farmhouse in the town of Stark where they raised six children and made cheese for a living. In 1890, her husband passed away, after fifty-five years of marriage. Delina's youngest son and his family moved in with her, remaining for another thirty-three years. In 1923, Delina, her son and his family moved to the town of Warren. Then 108 years old, Delina was in excellent health for a centenarian. Her only age-related ailment was hearing loss, but her mental faculties remained sharp, and she insisted on getting around without help, dressing herself and making her own bed each morning.

According to the Spring 1980 *Leatherstocking Journal*, Delina's great-grandchildren remembered her fondly. She wore the same style of clothing each day—a long dark dress and white apron—and she typically sat next to the hot woodstove in her favorite chair, often sleeping there contentedly through the night. She passed her memories of her lifetime onto her descendants, telling them, for example, how she remembered when candles were used exclusively, and then kerosene lamps, and finally Edison's first light bulb. She also recalled baking pies for the Indians in the newly settled town to appease them so they would let her sons be.

Other memorable occasions of her life included taking her first ride in a car on her 100th birthday and receiving a congratulatory letter from President Calvin Coolidge on her 112th birthday.

Then at 113 years of age, Leona Bell Jacobs, a famous New York City artist, was commissioned by Owen D. Young to paint a portrait of

Delina which was then displayed in the Canajoharie Library and Art Gallery and the Owen D. Young Central School. A few months later, on December 4, 1928, Delina passed away at her grandson's home in Richland Springs, Otsego County. The location of her gravesite in the middle of the Van Hornesville Cemetery overlooking the village green reminds visitors of the humble woman and gentle soul who lived the quintessential full life.

The Stone Baby

Frankfort

Talk about weird. In 1852, a 77-year-old woman in Frankfort died, and her autopsy revealed a calcified fetus about eight and a half months old that had died in her womb forty years earlier. They called it "the Stone Baby" of Herkimer County. Its scientific name is lithopedion, which, according to *The American Heritage Stedman's Medical Dictionary* is a "dead fetus, usually extrauterine, that has become calcified."

By all accounts, Mrs. Amos Eddy was an unusual woman. At age twenty-seven, seven years after marrying, Mrs. Eddy became pregnant and exhibited all the usual symptoms of pregnancy. Dr. William H. H. Parkhurst, her physician for the last ten years of her life, later wrote in a paper that Mrs. Eddy experienced "nausea and occasional vomiting, and many other symptoms which usually accompany this important change of system," including the miraculous fluttering of life within her as the pregnancy progressed. In that sense, the pregnancy had been completely normal, and the usual outcome was greatly anticipated, especially by Mr. Eddy who kept his horse and buggy ready for the big moment to arrive.

However, at eight and a half months, Mrs. Eddy suffered a mishap which would change the course of her pregnancy and become "one for the record books." The pot of dinner hanging over the fire tipped and spilled into the fireplace as she was tending to it, causing an immediate reflexive action. Even though Mrs. Eddy wasn't injured by the hot contents, the brief moment of panic was a jolt to her fragile system—such a jolt that she went into labor a couple of hours later. The doctor ordered

Courtesy of *Adirondack* by Barney Fowler

Photo of "stone" fetus

her to bed, keenly aware that every additional week of pregnancy was important to a successful birth. Everyone was relieved when the labor pains disappeared by the next morning, and they assumed she would make it to her due date, after all. But the due date came and went. Weeks passed by, then months, and Mrs. Eddy's health began to fail. Because there was no such thing as an ultrasound to confirm a pregnancy or the viability thereof, doctor upon doctor agreed that it must have been some "peculiar growth of the uterus," rather than a fetus, according to Parkhurst. He said, "None could believe it to be a child. Month after month rolled away, and at the expiration of about one year and a half, [Mrs. Eddy's] health began to improve; though the bulk of abdomen, which had been very large, did not diminish but little…"

Even though her health and vigor eventually returned, Mrs. Eddy never lost her pregnant shape and continued to have occasional bouts of labor pains for the rest of her life. The surprising post mortem exam in 1852 was conducted in the presence of about 20 witnesses, including a Utica newspaper reporter, who said:

"To the utter astonishment of all present, a full grown child was found, encased in a sort of bony or cartilaginous structure, except one leg and foot, and one elbow, which were almost entirely ossified." The sex of the six-pound baby was never determined, but the lithopedion was donated to the Albany Medical College museum and was, at one time, used in the study of anatomy and pathology.

Spectacular Spooks

Shadow Chasers

Potsdam, Hopkinton, Massena

Phillip Creighton always had an interest in the paranormal, but his curiosity was piqued six years ago when an Appalachian folklore class required him to go out in the field and speak to real people about their beliefs, including one old woman who shared some very interesting Appalachian tales (though not nearly as interesting as what Phillip would soon experience for himself). When he arrived at SUNY Potsdam, a friend who was aware of his interest in such things (as well as his growing stash of ghost-hunting paraphernalia) asked him to investigate "Bernie the Ghost." Word soon got out, and that investigation led to others, and before he knew it, Phillip was being asked to do seminars on ghost-hunting twice a semester! An Anthropology/Folklore and Archaeology Major with a minor in Geology, and a concentration in Photography, he is the founder, senior lead investigator, and senior researcher of a group of like-minded students from Potsdam, Remsen, Watertown, and Cicero. Their collective knowledge on the subject is as impressive as the array of technologically advanced equipment they have accumulated for use on investigations. They are Shadow Chasers: Paranormal Investigations & Research.

The members of Shadow Chasers include Phillip, who is also a regular columnist for SUNY Potsdam's student-run newspaper, *The Raquette*, and an up-and-coming author of a paranormal series based on his actual cases; newest member Katharine (Kate) Heuser, an investigator and researcher from Remsen, New York, who is a Psychology and Criminal Justice major; Brent Kelley, investigator and senior lead technician from

Cicero, New York, who is an Archaeology major; Mallory Albert, lead investigator and lead researcher from Cicero, who is an Art and History major; Lenore Gentner, senior lead investigator and researcher, who is an Archaeology major; and Amalie Meyers, lead communications medium and researcher, who is an Anthropology and Art History major. Together, this ambitious group of college students is a force to be reckoned with. They are the regional representatives for MAJDA, a paranormal research society and the International Ghost Hunters Society (IGHS). Their services are free and confidential.

After being solicited, the team of savvy investigators visits the site, interviews witnesses, sets up their equipment (including camcorders, voice recorders, and a plethora of other gadgets I'll get to in a moment) records atmospheric conditions, and then splits up into pairs to cover the area. If an anomalous reading is discovered or something unexpected and unusual occurs, the other team members converge to the active area with their respective gear to see if their own readings support the anomaly or can trace it to a more common source.

One of the first places the team ever investigated together was Knowles Hall—a residence hall near the Crane School of Music at SUNY Potsdam. Allegedly, in the seventies, a female student committed suicide by hanging herself from a railing. The janitorial staff found her body and quickly sealed the building while authorities whisked the body away before anyone saw it. Today, students claim to hear doors slamming and other unexplained noises. EVPs taken at the site have almost always revealed murmured voices that can't be accounted for. And near the old cafeteria in Knowles, Electromagnetic field (EMF) meters spiked in mid-air, for no obvious reason—potentially a sign that spirit energy may be present.

Satterlee Hall, one of the oldest buildings on campus, proved even more interesting than Knowles. In a third floor storage area, the crew picked up "somewhat erratic" EMF readings, indicating a possible haunting. But erratic EMF readings in and of themselves are not indicative of paranormal activity, unless all other possible sources of energy fields have been ruled out.

In the Satterlee Hall case, some of the members, including Phillip, got "zapped" by a strong energy field in mid-air, presumably paranormal in

Courtesy of Shadow Chasers

Phillip Creighton, Founder of Shadow Chasers

nature, while attempting to retrieve the audio recorder they had placed in the costume room just ten minutes earlier. But it was worth the jolt (easy for me to say), because in that short period of time, some phenomenal EVP recordings were captured from within the unoccupied room, and it didn't come from the spirit of the old woman students have seen in there. It was the sound of a little dog growling or yelping, and it wasn't an isolated incident. It was heard again a month later when the team checked again, and in one recording, the sound occurred five times. Interestingly, a student admitted that she had to leave the room one day after standing on a chair to retrieve something; she had heard a dog bark and got spooked. It was her account that enticed the team to check out that room. Another interesting thing Phillip noticed about the room is that as soon as he entered it, his radio frequency (RF) meter went off, but it stopped the second he walked out of the door. In fact, if he so much as put his foot or hand into the room—just a hand alone—it went off. It was as if the spirit in the room could use living bodies as antennae of sorts.

As exciting as the college jaunts (and haunts) sound, local cemeteries practically handed evidence of paranormal activity to the Shadow Chasers on a silver platter. At an old cemetery in Hopkinton, for example, members watched as an odd mist rolled across the road and back again at dusk, and they took an amazing photograph (see below) of a phantom tombstone. In the photograph, a long stick reaches horizontally across the back of several tombstones, but when it gets to the stone on the far right, it can be seen right through the stone. It's as if the stone is transparent. And what's more, the stone itself doesn't even exist! After the film was developed and the anomaly was discovered, the Shadow Chasers went back to the scene and discovered that there was no such tombstone.

Courtesy of Shadow Chasers

Mystery tombstone (to the far right) does not actually exist

Another photograph taken at the cemetery also seemed to reveal a phantom stone, which looked like it was encapsulated in a bubble (page 75). It could also be an orb in motion, but since the graveyard already had revealed one very obvious phantom stone, it's plausible that there were others. Pretty amazing stuff, but most amazing of all was the ghost that got the last laugh.

When the members were lightheartedly teasing each other, as they often do, and Mallory was holding the handy-dandy smog detector, they discovered that they weren't the only ones laughing. The smog detector (which looks like a Star Trek beaming device) emitted what could best be described as "pulsating laughter," as if a ghost were standing amongst the team members, laughing right along with them. If that isn't enough ghostly antics from one cemetery for you, read on.

Pine Grove #1 Cemetery on Beach Street in Massena has become quite well known for its supernatural occurrences. First there was the

Courtesy of Shadow Chasers

Orb in motion or phantom tombstone?

story of Dragon Obretenoff from my second book, *More Haunted Northern New York*. He was the star of a story about a ghost that whispered "turn around" to an unsuspecting cemetery visitor who, of course, did not turn around! Dragon's tombstone is at the rear of the cemetery, on the farthest road back…precisely the spot that the Shadow Chasers were investigating the night the cops showed up. Phillip and his team had set up all of their equipment for a full investigation and then they paired off into two groups who went in different directions. It wasn't long before a couple of local cops showed up on their nightly cemetery patrol. Little did they know they were about to walk right into a ghost trap…well, sort of. The Shadow Chasers had set up a digital voice recorder (DVR) with the audio amplifier on a tripod—it looks like a little clear satellite dish—towards the rear of the cemetery, where most of the activity seemed to be occurring. The contraption allows one to listen, via earphones, to ghostly chatter taking place near the DVR while they are some distance away. But instead of ghostly chatter, they heard Massena's finest circling around the device asking each other what it was—practically putting their faces right into the amplifier—so they were coming in very loud and clear! Phillip was probably stifling a grin as he made his way toward the curious duo. Along with Brent, he pulled out his ID badge and told them they were paranormal investigators. With that, one of the cops said, "You should be here at 3 A.M. if you want to catch something." The policeman proceeded to tell him about two officers who were on routine patrol near the cemetery one night when their

75

radio went "all funky." The other officers back at the station had a good laugh about it...until the same thing happened to two more officers. Apparently, their radio frequencies have been known to scroll all the way up, then all the way down again when in the vicinity of the grave-yard. Just before they left the crew, one of the officers added that she had seen "shadow people" going through the cemetery. It wouldn't be long before the investigators would understand what she meant, and they would even capture a possible culprit on film.

Everyone in the group had memorable experiences their second night at Pine Grove. For one thing, the freshly-charged batteries on the camcorder died instantly right near the two storage buildings at the back of the cemetery, much to the dismay of their camera man, Brent. A short time later, Lenore and Phillip were joking about the "Ghost Hunters" show on television and how it's funny to see the stars of that hit series actually chasing ghosts (running), when all of a sudden, they both heard a loud "Psst!" in their ears. At the same time, Phillip's faithful static monitor made a "Psst!" static sound at full power. Other members of the group reported sounds of someone running after them, even though nobody was. About that same time, Mallory and Kate became nauseated—a sign of exposure to high electromagnetic fields, which may cause lighthead-edness, nausea and dizziness. The rest of the group experienced nausea, to some degree or other, as well, but it didn't discourage them from con-tinuing their investigation.

Phillip was paired with Lenore, and just as he looked toward the end of the road at the back of the cemetery, which is lit by a streetlight on the corner, his attention was drawn to the streetlamp itself. It seemed to be pulsing between dim and bright. As he neared it, he saw what looked like the silhouette or shadow of a person, but with no solid person any-where in sight. The shadow person suddenly darted from under the light toward the cemetery, and as it did, the streetlamp brightened again. Phillip brought Lenore to the area, just as "the shadow" ran back. They both watched, transfixed, as the figure darted to the light and away again, as if toying with its audience. Then they noted that the bulb had obviously been replaced, because the bulbs on other streetlamps nearby were yellowish, and this one was a bright white (or a dim white, depend-ing on whether or not a ghost was under it). Phillip called the entire group over, but the shadow was playing shy. Only when it had an audience of one or two would it come out to play. When the whole group was together, nothing happened; but when just two at a time stayed to watch, they could see it—and actually hear it! It made a swishing sound as it darted past them. Phillip suggested that perhaps it was feeding off his group's energy fields, because the longer they stood around watching it, the faster the figure became. It also was obviously depleting the energy from the streetlamp as well—which explained the flickering and pulsating of the light, and which also probably explains why the bulb on that particular streetlamp required replacement, when the other streetlamps nearby didn't.

An extraordinary photo taken at Pine Grove right next to Dragon Obretenoff's stone showed what appeared to be an apparition of a man walking toward the road from the gravestones. The misty anomaly in the photo revealed the side angle of a man's upper and lower body. Was that their shadow person? The black and white reproduction of the actual photograph for publication does not do it justice, but it gives you an idea (below).

Amalie Meyers, a young and gifted psychic intuitive, believes that their group was dealing with at least two spirits, not one, during their investigation. She doesn't feel they had anything to do with Dragon Obretenoff. In one instance, as she walked around while another group member was taking photographs of her, she paused and said, "I can feel something

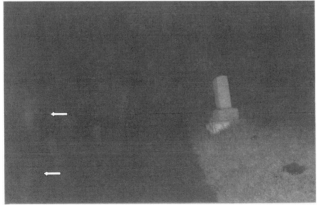

Courtesy of Shadow Chasers

Misty figure stepping onto road at cemetery

here." Sure enough, the photograph yielded Amalie standing just several feet away from an orb she couldn't see with the naked eye (you usually can't), yet she was looking right toward it (below). It wasn't the first time her feeling of a presence has been backed up by a photograph of an orb.

Courtesy of Shadow Chasers

Amalie correctly identifying an orb right in front of her

After several hours, feeling drained and a bit nauseated, the group packed up their equipment and prepared to leave; but not before experiencing one last supernatural incident. Lenore heard a distinct running sound that came toward her, passed straight through her car, and then could be heard continuing on behind her. Yep, it was definitely time to call it a night.

If something of a scientific nature is responsible for strange happenings, the Shadow Chasers will find it. After meeting with them recently, I invited them into my one-hundred-year-old Victorian house so I could see them in action. I hadn't expected them to find anything, and it was an impromptu walk-through, so they didn't utilize all of their equipment, just their EMF and RF meters and the Electro Smog Detector. In the two months since we bought the house, we've only had a few minor incidents that we haven't been able to explain—a TV turning itself on at 3 A.M., a series of bumping noises one night in the dining room, the sound of footsteps in the stairway, and a photograph falling off the wall in a very unusual manner. But, I have to admit, the baffling readings the investigators got from the second they walked through my back door left us all scratching our heads in bewilderment...and eager to do a follow-up investigation, with more manpower and more equipment.

The basement was clear—meaning no unexplainable electromagnetic or radiation fields. But the main doors, both front and back, caused high EMF readings that could not be explained. And the rear door, which we consider the main entrance, only picked up EMF on the inside part of the door. Outside, it was clear. It's as if the second you walk in that door, an energy field is activated. The front door, the original solid wood door, also set off all of the EMF meters. Mallory theorized that perhaps a previous owner had the entranceways blessed, according to their religious beliefs, and the blessing was so powerful that it created an energy field of protection around the doorways that can actually be detected by sensitive equipment such as theirs. (I like that theory. The house does have a very protective feel to it.)

Photo by author

My house

In the living room—a large open area with high ceilings and six windows—the EMF meters went crazy, picking up a wall-to-wall energy field that was at first near the ceiling, and then it seemed to drift downward, so that the meters were beeping at chest height rather than overhead. It was as if the entire room was magnetized or activated, setting off meters and beepers of every member. Kate was using an EMF meter which spiked and remained elevated directly under an end table in one corner of the living room, on the original hardwood floor near the front window. Nothing in the basement below the living room floor could explain such an abnormally high reading, which was isolated to that one very specific tiny area under the end table. Unusual readings continued in almost every room of my three-story house—there was even an electro-magnetic charge given off by a wedding ring set and blanket that belonged to my boyfriend's mother who passed away a year and a half ago. If EMFs can indicate spirit energy, then it's comforting to know his mother was likely right there with us, causing the reaction. As far as the rest of the house goes, were the erratic readings simply caused by old wiring in a house so old? Or was it evidence of paranormal activity?

The house is so comfortable and beautiful that I couldn't really blame anyone for wanting to "share" it with us, whether we are able to see them or not. Maybe we'll have more answers after the follow-up investigation at my house. Stay tuned for the results, along with more of the investi-gators' adventures, in the sequel to this book to be released in the future.

Gesundheit!

Malone

Photo by Stephanie Demers. Courtesy of M. Spicer

The Spicer home, Malone

Marc and Sarah Spicer viewed dozens of houses in Malone before they finally found the one for them four years ago. From the moment they walked through the door of the 180-year-old house at 19 Wellington Street, they knew they belonged there. A week after moving in, they married on the back deck. Six months passed uneventfully, and then...

It was early one morning in the spring of 2003, when Marc Spicer was awakened by a hearty sneeze coming from downstairs. Not a big deal, unless you're certain you're the only one home. Sarah was visiting her parents, and Marc's son, who is now six, was with his ex-wife. It was just Marc and their two cats; and, yet, the sound that woke him from his slumber was definitely a loud sneeze from a man, and it definitely came from somewhere below his second-floor bedroom. Marc sat up and grabbed the cordless phone. He asked the police officer he called to stay on the line while he searched the house, because he was certain someone had broken in. Both embarrassed and relieved to find nobody there, he apologized and told the officer that it must have been a vivid dream. Even though he couldn't explain what he'd heard, it hadn't even registered at that time that his house could be haunted. It would take a lot more than a sneeze to convince Marc of something he'd never really believed in; and, sure enough, there just so happened to be a lot more where "that" came from.

When their daughter was born in the spring of 2004, the Spicers were in the process of remodeling several rooms, but it wasn't until about a year later when several home improvement projects were well under way that the unexplained phenomena really kicked in. They saw, for example, shadowy movement in one particular corner of a room upstairs that they call the reading room. Surprisingly, their two grown cats are especially fond of that spot and are constantly drawn to it, even when boxes and other items make it difficult to get to. If there is a spirit presence in that corner, it must be an animal lover...or a young child. Pets are inherently drawn to children. And Marc & Sarah had heard the pitter-patter of little feet running across the upstairs when the entire Spicer family, cats and all, was downstairs in the living room. Their daughter, now two, has been pointing and speaking to what she calls "nice baby" and "pretty baby" since she began to talk. This always happens at the top of the stairs, just outside their daughter's bedroom door—a psychic later confirmed there is a spirit of a child in the home. Sometimes their daughter reaches out her little hand "as if to caress the baby's face," according to Marc, and says excitedly, "Hello, Baby!" whenever she sees it.

One night Marc woke up to the sound of a woman calling, "Jane!" Assuming he was hearing things, he fell back to sleep, but was quickly awakened again to the same woman calling out the same name. The windows were all closed, it was the middle of the night, and the voice was in his house. It sounded, he said, like "a concerned mother calling for her child." Like the time that he heard the mysterious sneeze, he got up, searched his house from top to bottom, and found nobody. The next morning, still shaken by the entire incident, he was dressing his daughter—not even two years old at the time—when she called out in her wee little voice, "Jane! Jane!" She repeated the same words with the same inflection that Marc had heard, meaning she had heard the same thing he had. Was "Jane" the pretty baby the Spicer's daughter kept encountering in the hallway? If so, perhaps the woman calling to her from beyond was her mother, grandmother, or maybe a nanny.

There were other things, as well. Sometimes Marc and Sarah could hear hammering and whistling from somewhere in the house—they still do, in fact. Marc woke up at precisely 2:52 A.M. several mornings in a row, and their daughter woke up screaming at exactly midnight for several days in a row. Their son acts nervous about going upstairs alone, even though the couple has never spoken of their house possibly being haunted in front of the children, and the boy doesn't seem to even know why he's nervous. Marc has heard his name whispered in the middle of the night, and objects have come up missing and then reappeared in a very obvious location some time later.

The bathroom seems to be a hotspot of inexplicable phenomena. Both Marc and Sarah have watched as the two upstairs bathroom doors opened and closed right before their eyes. The doors are secured evenly and require an actual push or pull to move them. Sarah has often experienced dizziness in the bathroom; and, I have to admit, I felt it myself when I visited them prior to writing this story, quite strongly, in fact. The feeling is most intense at the back of the shower. Not long ago, Marc said, "A strange sewer-like smell emanated from under one of the two upstairs bathroom sinks." They asked several plumbers and contractors to try to find the source, but nobody was able to. Fortunately, the smell disappeared after a very talented psychic investigator named Belle Salisbury went through their house in July 2006. Belle owns The Whispering Willow shop in downtown Massena and is featured prominently in my third book, *Still More Haunted Northern New York*.

Belle's visit to the Spicer home answered a lot of questions and confirmed much of what the couple had already come to suspect about their house. The psychic, flanked by two students, was not given any details about the Spicers' experiences when she first arrived for the investigation. She prefers telling it as she sees it without any preconceived notions, so she starts with a clean slate. A bathroom seems like a strange place to start an investigation, but Belle was immediately drawn to it, so up the stairs they went. As far as the Spicers were concerned, it made perfect sense that a psychic would head straight to the bathroom, since that was hands-down the most active room in the house (in a paranormal sense). Belle would soon explain the full extent of its activity. Flanked by two of her more gifted students, the psychic pointed into the room and asked the Spicers if either of them had ever experienced dizziness in there. When Sarah admitted she often did, Belle pointed to the back of the shower—much to the Spicers' amazement—and said there was a "vortex" (doorway from this world to the next) in the shower itself. Heightened spirit activity around such doorways is known to be a huge drain on the energy of individuals standing on or near them, especially if the spirits require energy to manifest (reveal themselves).

The next stop was the Spicers' little girl's room. At exactly the spot that their daughter stops and "pats" the baby outside of her bedroom door, Belle said she felt the presence of an 18-month-old girl there. She also felt the presence of a spirit at the back of the room—an older lady who served as a nanny to the child—where one of her students stood, swaying back and forth. Belle said a rocking chair had once been in that corner, and the Spicers agreed they had a rocking chair there at one time; but it's more likely that Belle sensed the rocking chair the nanny had used, since she was in the process of discerning the nanny and child spirits in, or near, that room. It's generally felt by all that the nanny was likely the voice Marc heard saying "Jane!" that night, and it's also likely that the eighteen-month-old child is Jane. Belle feels the child succumbed to illness, as she was not a healthy presence. Interestingly, a picture of the garage seems to reveal a toddler's face in the reflective material of the garbage can.

The other spirits Belle sensed were in the Reading Room, where the Spicers have seen shadowy movements, and on the back deck. One is a handyman type, very tall and very frail. That could explain the hammering and whistling sounds, as well as the sneeze. And there is a teenage boy, not related to the house or its people, but he has ties to the land and passes through sometimes. Belle believes he was killed long ago in a

Courtesy of M. Spicer

Image of toddler face on garbage can

farming accident when the area was still farmland.

As soon as Belle left that day, the putrid smell from the upstairs bathroom disappeared. Sometimes, once a spirit has been acknowledged, they stop trying to get attention. That may be what happened there. She said all four spirits would most likely leave if asked to, but the Spicers see no reason to ask them to leave. Marc said, they've accepted them as part of the house and even find them comforting to have around, in a sense. In fact, one night when he was awakened by unidentified sounds, he got up to check on their children and found his daughter had a blanket wrapped too tightly around her neck, so he removed the blanket, and still thanks the helpful spirit for awakening him. They still hear things, and objects still come up missing, but Belle told them those sorts of incidents will probably stop once the home improvement is finished. For now, the Spicers are content to coexist with the spirits and are no longer afraid of them. He said, "How could we ask them to leave? This house has been their home a lot longer than it has been ours."

Crane School Student Haunting

Potsdam

Brian and his friends are not the types to play practical jokes on each other. They go to the Crane School of Music at SUNY Potsdam and are every bit as proper, reserved, and organized as you would expect future composers or great instrumentalists to be.

So just what created the chaos in their kitchen one evening in March 2006 is still a mystery. Brian lives in one of the old Clarkson family homes on Leroy Street, and the house is said to be haunted; though by whom, nobody knows. On the evening in question, Brian and his roommate, Marc, had a few of their close friends over "just to relax and prepare for the coming school week." When it was time to leave, Brian and several of his friends pulled out of the driveway first, and then Marc followed right behind them with the remaining friends who needed a ride back to campus. One of the students in Brian's car commented on how it was odd that Marc had forgotten to turn off the light in his room, because they all knew how conscientious he was about turning it off whenever he left the house, even for a short time, and they knew he wasn't planning to return home right away. But that wasn't nearly as odd as the light turning off by itself just as they were discussing it, even though everyone had already left the house. They figured a bulb must have blown or something.

Brian returned home a short time later, unlocked the door and took his shoes off on the doormat, then proceeded into the kitchen to read the unopened mail on the counter. That's when he saw that every single cabinet and drawer was wide open. He said, "The drawers were almost falling on the floor. I freaked out and froze with fear, and then decided that I had better grab the biggest kitchen knife I have in case someone had broken in." But there were no signs of a break-in. He had to unlock the front door as always when he came home. He quickly called the friends he had just dropped off to see if any of them had done it, even though he already knew they hadn't. So he told them he was on his way back to their place. As he moved cautiously toward the front door, he noticed that the closet was also opened, so he closed it quickly and left. By the time he got to campus, his friends had already called everyone else who had been at the house that night to make sure none of them were at fault. They recalled that the last person in the kitchen said he had only poured a glass of water before they left, and they would have heard him doing more than that.

Brian's friend, Dana, called her brother who is an undercover policeman who told them to meet him back at the house. They went through the house thoroughly, searching for signs of intruders or missing items, and found neither. Granted, the policemen were trained in finding intruders you can actually see and feel. Too distraught and mystified to stay there that night, Brian and Marc slept elsewhere but returned the next morning to get their books and take a shower. Marc left before Brian. Once again alone in the house, Brian had another unexplainable experience. He turned the faucet in the bathtub off tightly when he was done showering, because the showerhead would otherwise continue dripping. But as he was preparing to leave the house, he heard a noise in the bathroom and went to see what it was. Five streams of water were shooting out of the showerhead—not dripping—streaming. Again, he turned the shower off tightly and left with no further ado.

As with many old homes in Potsdam that are now occupied by students, the house on Leroy Street has an apparent occasional intruder with a motive not usually apparent.

Haunted Staircase

Plattsburgh

If I had to pinpoint which architectural feature of a building is most often associated with ghostly phenomena, I'd have to say staircases are at the top of my list. Nearly every ghost story I've heard mentions stairs: a ghost at the top of the stairs, ghostly footsteps going up or down the stairs, animals growling at something unseen on the staircase or landing, dark shadows slithering up and down the stairs, persistent cold spots in the stairway, and so on. Unfortunately, one of the more common themes involving ghosts and staircases has people being thrown down the stairs by unseen hands, sometimes repeatedly.

In 1996, Debbie was living in an old rented farmhouse on Stafford Road in Plattsburgh with her husband and two daughters. From the start, she noticed that the stairs leading to the second floor always "felt strange." She admitted they had all taken turns with unexplainable tumbles down the stairs, leaving them bruised, not to mention confused. Their dog may have sensed that something bad happened in the stairs— or that something bad actually lived in or on the stairs—because she hated going near them. The dog seemed to feel duty-bound to follow its family up or down the stairs, but she inevitably growled the whole way, even though she was very friendly anywhere else in the home. The family actually has pictures of the dog growling in the stairway.

Debbie recalls a day when her husband was napping upstairs, and her youngest daughter was in her bedroom. Debbie was in the living room watching TV when, all of a sudden, she heard a loud noise—someone or something falling down the stairs, landing at the bottom, and hitting the door with a thud. Dreading what she would find, she raced to the stairs and looked at the landing, but nobody was there. At the same time, her daughter peeked around the corner at the top of the stairs and asked Debbie what had fallen down the stairs. Even though there was no physical evidence of anything having fallen, they both clearly heard the same thing. They looked all around the house and in the basement but never learned the source of the sound.

In every one of my books in the *Haunted Northern New York* series, there are stories that involve strange activity and noises in staircases. Numero uno is obviously the sound of mysterious footsteps going up or down stairs, since that is one of the most common signs of a haunting (if not the most), but second place is the sound of something falling or rolling down the stairs. I've heard such sounds described as a person tumbling, or a person's head rolling down the stairs (morbid, but true), a loud bowling ball crashing toward the landing, or even just a ping pong ball bouncing lightly down. And, unless it's an actual person taking a tumble, the source for the sound is rarely found—which is probably a good thing, considering the aforementioned possibilities.

The Watcher

Hermon

Most people who live in homes they believe are haunted become accustomed to the strange happenings and feel no urgency to move out on account of the ghosts. However, those who have had terrifying ordeals—which are thankfully few and far between—often pack up and move away quickly, bearing a life-long dread of ever returning. Donna shared a story about a house she lived in near Hermon, and the premise was all too familiar to me. She explained that while she was recently up this way for a visit, she pulled into the driveway of the vacant house she lived in forty-five years ago, but she instantly became so spooked—even though it was a bright, sunny day—that she found herself backing out of the driveway and driving off as fast as she could, feeling all the while that some unseen and horrible presence was following, or watching, her. I can't tell you how many times I've heard people talk of similar experiences.

These people have dreams and nightmares their entire lives about the purportedly haunted house they once lived in, as if it's a never-ending struggle to overcome the fear that the house instilled in them. Yet they feel strangely drawn back to look at the house from the street—like a bizarre test of a fear they must conquer—and, inadvertently, they end up fleeing again and again with a feeling that the house or something in it remembers them and knows they are back, within grabbing distance. They literally feel like there is something evil watching them as they drive off that would like nothing better than to get them. That's why so many people get physically sick and fearful as they approach or pass by a house that holds terrifying memories from their past.

Donna remembers often seeing a man looking down at her mother as she slept when her father (a truck driver) was away on a run. Donna's mother had the entire family sleep in her room every time their father was away. But her mother wasn't the only one being watched by an uninvited presence. Donna's sister once awakened and saw the man peering down at Donna as she slept. And Donna encountered a woman dressed all in black at the top of the stairs one day when she was home sick. The woman, whom Donna swears she'll never forget, had "the most evil look on her face" as she drifted toward the bedroom at the top of the stairs. Donna, unable to move while witnessing the apparition, understood why her dog had been snarling just seconds before. Once the woman at the top of the stairs was no longer in view, Donna pulled herself together enough to run outside with her dog until her mother returned from work. The family moved to Carthage soon after, and although they've had other paranormal experiences, nothing has ever frightened them the way the house in Hermon did. Perhaps the evil apparition at the top of the stairs was somehow responsible for the family's many unexplained falls down those same stairs. And perhaps she and her male companion who likes to watch people sleep are still there waiting for Donna to return. Maybe they really were watching her when she pulled up to the house.

Ghost Party at the Motel!

Massena

I receive a lot of e-mails from people wanting to share their supernatural experiences with me, but this next story really caught my interest, because the e-mail began like this: "I am your typical Army Sergeant with a pretty level head and an explanation for everything…" I knew it had to be a good one, and it was, but the people involved are still in the military, so they requested that I not use their real names.

"Bud" explained to me that shortly after the 9/11 attacks, his team who worked with Customs and Border Protection (CBP), began touring the state ports of entry. They were stationed out of Buffalo and had been on the road for about a month when the incident at Massena occurred. It was early November 2001, and Massena was the last stop on their tour—and undoubtedly their most memorable. Because of a snafu in their motel reservations, when Bud and his team arrived at the motel where the rest of their contingent was staying, they were told that there were no more openings. The officer in charge told the four of them to choose any other motel in town to stay at for the week, so they stopped at the first place they came upon, which will also remain anonymous. (Not all businesses want to be known as haunted.) They each got their room keys, and Bud's room was between the rooms of his friends, Mark and Mary, on the second floor.

Shortly after unpacking, Mary showed up at Bud's door complaining about the "party" going on upstairs, directly over her room, but when they stopped talking to listen, all was silent. Just as Mary was commenting on how strange it was that neither he nor Mark had complained about the party she heard, Mark showed up from the room on the other side of Bud's and started complaining about the loud music above HIS room. All three were puzzled by the fact that Bud's room was silent, but the rooms on either side were very noisy. They decided to hang out in Bud's room and order Italian food to be delivered. Mark and Bud agreed to go pick up some beer, but Bud was quick to point out that none of them had been drinking prior to that point. Mary would stay behind to wait for the food. As the men got into the van, they looked back up at the room and Bud said, "Hey, Mark, didn't you say you heard the party over your room?" Mark went completely pale when Bud said, "We're on the top floor."

They continued on their way, unaware that things were about to get even stranger. When they left, Mary had been wearing purple shorts and a light blue t-shirt. But when Mark and Bud pulled back into their parking space, they saw the delivery man standing outside of Bud's door with Mary who had changed into blue jeans and a light blue sweatshirt. Just as Bud was thinking about it, Mark said, "Hm. Mary must have changed." On their way up the stairs, they passed the delivery man, but nobody else. As they entered Bud's room, Mary was lying on the bed wearing her shorts and t-shirt! The men looked at each other before turning back to Mary and asking her if she had just changed really quickly. She hadn't. When they asked her who the girl was that looked just like her with the delivery guy, she said, "What girl?" Bud said, "The girl that was outside of this door, standing right next to the delivery guy!" Mary said nobody else had been there at all.

Shaken, Bud called the front desk, introduced himself and said, "Look, I'm not trying to sound weird or anything, but has anyone else reported anything strange going on in this motel?" The clerk replied curtly, "No!" and hung up. Okay, then. . . that's an affirmative. The next morning, just as the novelty of staying in a genuinely haunted hotel began to sound kind of neat, the lieutenant, whose room was in a different part of the motel altogether, ordered them all to pack their things. They were moving to another hotel at once. When the three complained that they wanted to stay, she said she didn't care, they were leaving "Now!" From the urgency in her voice, they assumed that she must have had her own experience and wasn't taking any ifs, ands, or buts about it.

The BrightSide on Raquette

Raquette Lake

A couple checked into a hotel on Indian Point in Raquette Lake more than a hundred years ago. In the middle of a blizzard, the man set out across the frozen lake for the village. He never made it; and he never returned. And his wife has never left. After his disappearance, she kept a silent vigil by the window of their guestroom, awaiting his return. The only thing that ever pulled her away from her vigil was the sound of the piano playing in the Great Room. As it was in the past, so it still remains; for many claim the heartbroken woman's spirit still haunts the room above the kitchen that she shared with her husband, and there are claims that she still makes an appearance when she hears someone playing the original Vose and Sons piano at the place that changed her life forever—The BrightSide on Raquette.

The above story is just one of the ghostly tales BrightSide, a vacation complex on Raquette Lake only accessible by boat, shares on its web site, www.brightsideonraquette.com. The 122-year-old Adirondack resort is a treasure-trove of history and hauntings. The resort was an intense labor of love for Joe and Mary Bryere, the couple who built it in the late 1800s. But no two people were better suited for the major undertaking, according to the web site. It says, "In terms of stamina, Joe and Mary were a good match. Mary could swing an axe and pull a crosscut saw on par with any man, and legend has it that Joe killed a 1,200-pound Bull Moose with his bare hands in his younger days in Canada."

By the time it opened as a hundred-acre vacation complex, The BrightSide consisted of the hotel, plus a number of cabins, a boathouse,

95

and a water tower. Besides all of the "modern conveniences" it boasted in 1891, the resort also offered golf, tennis, and water sports. Not only was Joe the builder, owner, and operator of The BrightSide, along with Mary, but he was also a sought-out carpenter whose Adirondack style furniture still graces The BrightSide compound, as well as the Adirondack Museum at Blue Mountain Lake. The tireless couple had bore and raised four children at The BrightSide and somehow managed to remain active in their community. Joe even served a stint as county coroner, back in the days when it was common practice to bury bodies in the loose soil of a basement when it was impossible to dig into the frozen ground outside.

The BrightSide enjoyed prosperity and recognition in its heyday and was a favorite resort of many wealthy guests and colorful characters, which was no doubt delightful for the Bryere children. But as time marched on, the children grew up and moved away. Joe had been running The BrightSide for fifty years when he passed away in 1941. His daughter Clara, a nurse in World War I in France, returned home upon word of her father's death, to run The BrightSide; as her mother Mary was, by that time, in no condition to do so herself, due to her advanced age. Every bit as capable as her parents, Clara not only continued to run The BrightSide for sixteen years, but she also made some much-needed improvements, earning her the nickname "Miss BrightSide." In 1957, when she sold the inn to BrightSide on Raquette Lake Incorporated, she donated many of her father's wooden creations to the Adirondack Museum at Blue Mountain Lake.

In 2001, a telecommunications firm—one of three owned by Frank Grotto, called The Light Connection, purchased the property. Under the direction of Grotto, modern plumbing, including several additional bathroom facilities, was established on each floor; propane furnaces replaced coal-burning furnaces; windows, foundations, and roofing were repaired or replaced; and new furnishings were brought in, to mix with the original antique pieces. A fresh coat of paint and a couple of new porches, and The BrightSide was good to go. The resort has since been used as a corporate training facility and for special events for Frank Grotto's companies. It is now also being offered to other companies and to private groups for the same purpose—company retreats, annual meetings, training seminars, and special events. The BrightSide is guaranteed to leave its guests with something to talk about—even if they don't have their own paranormal experience while there. And if they do have such an experience, there's a good chance it will happen in "The Ghost Room." That's right...one room, in particular, has been designated officially as The Ghost Room, and a running list of ghostly happenings at The BrightSide is posted outside of that room.

There was the young girl who decided to retire early to bed one night but changed her mind quickly after discovering that her bed was shaking as she lay in it. In fact, it was shaking so badly that she couldn't hold the book she was reading. Although she knew nothing of The BrightSide ghost stories, the rest of her group apparently did, and they wasted no time telling her that she wasn't the first person that had happened to in that room. (Nice that they waited to tell her that after the fact!) Another woman swore she heard her camera, which was on the other side of the room, snapping pictures one morning as she made her bed. A couple of weeks later, after she got her film developed, she was stunned to find three photographs, each taken from the exact same spot where the camera had been sitting that night, showing blue orbs. Think about that...it means a ghost was taking pictures of a ghost! Incidentally, the Mohawk Valley GhostHunters did an investigation of the grounds in August 2002, and they discovered a number of blue orbs in their photographs, as well. A copy of their report stating that the original building was found to be "very active" (paranormally) is available for all guests of The BrightSide to read.

Another guest was also witness to The BrightSide's blue orbs. He mentioned the bluish spheres he had watched in his room the night before at breakfast one day, telling his companions that he thought they must have been reflections off the lake from boat lights. The only problem was, he soon found out, his window didn't face the lake, or any source of water. Thinking it would make the concerned gentleman feel more comfortable, the staff told him he wasn't the first guest to see blue orbs in his room. But their words had the opposite effect. It convinced him to leave that very day!

At The BrightSide on Raquette, the list just goes on and on...

Techno-Ghost

Massena

By the time M.H. got married and moved to Massena, she was already primed for the paranormal experiences she was about to have. She had grown up in two haunted houses. The first was a gabled Victorian that her family lived in during the early sixties when she was a grade-schooler. The house was at one time so prominent that a sketch of its likeness can be found in the *History of St. Lawrence County* (1908). Although M.H.'s family only lived there for three years, her father endeavored to painstakingly restore the original features, spending many late nights in the woodshop portion of his basement. It was there that the family's first brush with the spirit world occurred.

It was past midnight, and M.H.'s father was, as usual, absorbed in his work on some pieces in the basement while everyone else was asleep. When he heard the door to the basement open, he assumed it was his wife coming down. He distinctly heard footsteps on the stairs, but when he looked up from his work, nobody was there. Even so, he knew he was not alone. The hair on the back of his neck had stood up, and he felt a very strong presence of someone who was deeply disturbed in the room with him. Mustering up his best commanding voice, he firmly said, "There is no sadness in this house. Go away!" And it listened.

M.H.'s mother also admitted to feeling like she wasn't alone, when she thought she was. She often heard unexplained footsteps, and on one occasion, just as she was about to turn on the vacuum cleaner, she heard footsteps scurrying away from her, as if in fear of the modern-day appliance.

The next house M.H. lived in didn't appear to be haunted until after

M.H. had moved out. Her mother's cousin was visiting her parents when she had a shocking encounter with a spirit, right in M.H.'s old bedroom. One night while the cousin was in bed reading, she glanced up to see an apparition standing at the foot of her bed—a woman who was wearing a long, old-fashioned dress. The ghost looked at the woman and said curtly, "Why are you in my room?" Before the poor houseguest could reply, the ghost simply vanished before her eyes. There were two known deaths on the property in the two hundred years since the old farmhouse was built—the drowning deaths of two of the original builder's sons at different times. But nobody knows who the ghost lady could be that was claiming the room as hers.

In the nineties, M.H. and her husband rented a house on S. Main Street in Massena. Her husband was doing software engineering over the Internet, so he was very familiar with computer diagnostics. But none of his expertise could help him diagnose his own computer's malfunction one night when the document he was typing in Word took on a life of its own, even with his hands resting in his lap. As he and M.H. sat watching in awe, a single letter from the document he had been working on was deleted, while simultaneously, two new letters were added. At other times, the two would be watching television as a "static" shadow drifted ominously across the screen, as if the electromagnetic field of the television were being disturbed; which is, in fact, exactly what happens when spirits (which have an Electromagnetic field all their own) are present.

As many people have discovered, pets are especially sensitive to spirit energy, and pets also return to their earthly surrounds after passing over sometimes, just as their deceased human counterparts do. M.H.'s cat saw something terrifying along the wall of her house one day that M.H. and her husband couldn't see. The cat stopped in its tracks staring at the blank wall, then darted away, crouching down low as it ran, as if it was afraid of something.

An Ogdensburg psychic walked through the house and, without knowing the home's history or about the strange happenings going on there, she quickly picked up on three spirits—a young boy, his dog, and a woman. None of the spirits, she said, had ever lived in the house. They just passed through it occasionally. This is something important to keep in mind…if you experience a haunting, it may only be an isolated incident involving a spirit who stops in just because it "happened to be in the neighborhood." The boy appeared to be six to eight years old, according to the psychic, and he was searching for his dog which was always one step ahead of him. The boy was fascinated by electronics and often paused long enough to approach the television or computer. That would explain the malfunctioning computer and television set. And the little dog spirit was staying with the boy for as long as it took for the boy to cross over…a faithful companion. The dog spirit explained the cat's odd behavior, because the only thing the cat didn't like was dogs! And it would explain the sensation of a dog or cat brushing up against M.H.'s husband's leg that he felt one night.

There was a jovial, neighborly woman who visited the house in spirit sometimes, simply because she enjoyed going from house to house sitting for a bit and having tea, even if the conversation was only one-sided. All in all, none of the spirits was a problem, except for perhaps the boy who unintentionally disrupted electronic devices on occasion. But the psychic told M.H. to talk to the boy the next time something like that happened, as if he were alive, and to ask him to please not touch the equipment. M.H. did just that, and it did seem to work.

Prelude to Freddy Krueger

Watertown

I've heard some pretty chilling stories about ghosts on dark back roads that seem to follow or chase passing cars. There was an alleged phantom haunting teens "along [a] lonely road" in the Watertown-Fort Drum region. It was reported in an unidentified newspaper clipping, dated June 22, 1960. The article's subtitle reads: "Apparition on Perch Lake Highway Follows Two Cars—Sheriff's Deputies Investigate." In this case, two visibly-shaken teenage girls reported to authorities that a mysterious hooded figure ran after the two cars they were riding in with six others down the Perch Lake Road northwest of Watertown, even as the cars reached speeds of fifty miles per hour. Because the girls seemed genuinely frightened and were trembling, sheriff's deputies took their report seriously—not necessarily expecting a phantom on the loose, but possibly a costumed prankster or someone projecting an image on the roadway with a movie projector. But if there was a prankster out there scaring drivers on dark roads, it could cause a serious accident, so the sergeant on duty told the young girls that they would question other witnesses and send someone "out there" to investigate.

The investigation and interviews revealed that one of the girls and her boyfriend, a Pfc. from Camp (Fort) Drum had seen the same hooded figure several weeks earlier, so they brought six skeptical friends along with them this time for an impromptu "ghost hunt." The cars, both driven by Pfc.'s from Fort Drum, were headed southwest on Perch Lake Road at 11:15 P.M., driving about twenty-five miles per hour, when presumably the same figure appeared out of nowhere by the side of the road, a half mile from Bradley Street. The first to see the figure were actually the people in the second car, so it flashed its headlights at the first car to alert them, and, at that time, both cars picked up speed to almost fifty-five miles per hour. All eight witnesses agreed that the figure looked like a middle-aged woman wearing a long, white nightgown with a hood. No facial features were discernible at all, and the figure made no sound.

Most alarming was the fact that one hand appeared to consist of just three long fingernails, rather than an actual hand itself...prelude to Freddy Krueger? Perhaps Wes Craven, creator of the wildly popular *Nightmare on Elm Street*, got his idea for the razor-fingered Krueger after reading this very newspaper article! It's no secret that, while Craven was a professor of Humanities at Clarkson University, a student film project in 1968 which spoofed horror films using scenes from Potsdam's Elm Street became the inspiration for his 1984 box-office smash. Had he read about the razor-fingered figure on the Perch Lake Road that terrified teens several years earlier? Maybe that was his inspiration for the character of Freddy Krueger.

At any rate, one of the girls who saw the figure said it moved like someone in an old-fashioned movie...kind of slow, choppy, and creepy. When it came between the two cars, the headlights from the second car shown right through it—meaning it was transparent. The witnesses said it was as if the figure were trying to force them off the road, going so far as to grab the side of one car. So much for the sheriff's deputy's theory of a movie projector image. The apparition chased the cars for a half mile, before vanishing just as they reached Bradley Street.

Another unsettling story I recall was about a group of teenagers on their way to a prom in the Watertown area in the seventies. They were driving down a dark road on the Tug Hill Plateau when they approached an odd-looking figure wearing a long gown and walking along the side of the road in the same direction as they were going. As they passed her, they decided it must be another student going to the prom, so they turned around to go back and offer a neighborly ride. This time, as they neared her, they noticed a deathly, almost menacing look in her eyes. Something wasn't right. The driver quickly spun around to drive away from the terrifying apparition, but as they sped down the road, they came upon the same figure, only this time the gruesome figure had somehow teleported herself in front of them and was heading right at them! Realizing this was a game they couldn't win, the driver gunned the car, leaving the ghost lady in its dust. They say prom night is a night to remember, and I'm sure those kids will never forget that one.

Strange Sites

Litchfield Castle

Tupper Lake

Courtesy of *Adirondack Album—Volume Two* by Barney Fowler

Photo of the Great Hall at Litchfield Castle

There are a lot of things I find remarkable about the Litchfield Castle, or Chateau, nestled in the mountains between Long Lake and Tupper Lake. But the reason I included it in a book about "weird" things is mainly because of the castle's Great Hall which displays hundreds of unusual animal mountings.

Edward H. Litchfield fell in love with the Adirondack wilderness as a young man who spent a lot of time camping and hunting in the region in the 1860s and 1870s. Then, as the wolf and cougar populations waned with the bounty law of 1871, Litchfield felt that the Adirondacks were no longer truly wild. He then tried his hand hunting in the Rockies, as well as in Europe, Asia, and Africa. His growing accumulation of exotic animal mountings was a testament of his excellent shooting abilities. But, like so many before him and so many since, the Adirondacks—though not still as wild as he preferred—was the only place he wanted to be. He had an idea.

Two years after marrying Madeleine Sands in Brooklyn, where Litchfield practiced law, the attorney purchased nine thousand acres of prime Adirondack property in the Towns of Altamont and Moody and called his property Litchfield Park. Today, Litchfield Park Corporation is a working estate involved in the wood products industry, and Litchfield Estate remains family-owned and private. But at the time Litchfield first purchased his land, he did it to satiate his hunter's appetite by stocking his own private forest preserve with exotic animals, as well as those in their natural habitats. Litchfield, who was obviously a man of great wealth and even greater dreams, stocked his new park with large numbers of fallow deer, moose, elk, wild boar, bears, jackrabbits, pheasants and beavers. Potsdam's *St. Lawrence Herald* of January 10, 1902, gave kudos to Litchfield's restocking efforts (even if they were for his own purposes). The article said:

"Quite a number of beavers have lately been purchased by E.H. Litchfield, proprietor of Litchfield Park near Tupper Lake and have been liberated on the waters of the park where it is expected they will soon begin their peculiar methods of house-cleaning and dam building."

The beavers were transported from North Dakota, and the article went on to say, "through the efforts of those gentlemen and other owners of private preserves, the Adirondacks may be once more stocked with valuable little animals." Unfortunately, Mr. Litchfield's dream of restocking his portion of the Adirondacks with wild things was never fully realized, because the eight-foot-high wire fencing he erected around the parameter of his compound was unable to withstand the harsh North Country elements and the vandalism by poachers. Nearly all of the animals he brought in either escaped through broken fence or were killed by poachers, or native species that had the upper hand.

According to *Historical Sketches of Franklin County and its Several Towns* (1918) by Frederick Seaver, the beavers were not killed off; in fact, they flourished. In 1911, Litchfield hired a New York City architect to design and construct a "hunting lodge" overlooking Jenkins Pond. But the lodge became a castle; and Jenkins Pond became Lake Madeleine, named after Litchfield's loving wife. As impressive as the so-called lodge, in and of itself, would be, there were many other details to tend to in order to make Litchfield Park a viable estate and retreat. For one thing, Litchfield needed to build miles of roads and drives leading to and around the remote site...otherwise, there would be no construction of anything! (Because the property is owned by Litchfield descendants who value their privacy, a five-mile private road that ends at the property's entrance gates is still the only means of access.) There was also a boathouse, a garage, and a stable to be built. But the crown jewel was definitely Litchfield Chateau, aka Litchfield Castle.

Stone for the three-to-six-foot walls throughout the chateau was quarried from nearby Mt. Morris. The stone walls ensured that the chateau was completely fireproof. Of the hundred or so rooms, there were few guest bedrooms, and there were originally just two bathrooms. The rest of the rooms included a number of living rooms, closets, halls, the kitchen, and the impressively flamboyant Great Hall. The Great Hall is. . .well, great—in more ways than one. Size-wise, it's sixty-five feet long by thirty feet wide and thirty feet high. The French medieval fireplace mantel is an incredible fifteen feet high. The walls are adorned with at least 160 hunting trophies—mounted heads and stuffed bodies of a variety of animals, both exotic and common.

By the time the chateau was completed and Litchfield and his son moved in, in 1913, Litchfield was so proud of his new "hunting lodge" and preserve that he opened Litchfield Park to the public. Fifteen years later, in 1928, the doors were closed to the public forever. Vandals and souvenir hunters had invaded his privacy and desecrated his property, even as he extended niceties to them. But Litchfield continued enjoying his piece of the Adirondack Park and ensured that future generations of the Litchfield family would, as well.

The Floating Islands

Colton

Many North Country residents have heard of Higley Flow, a man-made reservoir in South Colton created when a Central New York Power hydroelectric plant was built on the Raquette River in 1912. But did you ever hear of its floating islands? Like many man-made reservoirs of its kind, Higley Flow is now a state park consisting of a beach, boat launch, and campground and offering year-round outdoor recreational opportunities. But before most of the readers of this book were ever born, something remarkable took place at Higley Flow. Islands were born—floating islands—up to eleven acres in size. And they were creating a lot of problems for a lot of people; namely, shoreline property owners and power project operators. In response to the extraordinary natural marvel, a plan of action so ingenious was developed that it had never been attempted in Northern New York before, nor since. The story was mentioned in such prestigious magazines as *Scientific American*, *Popular Mechanics*, and *Popular Science*.

According to reporter Barney Fowler, the story began in 1914 when a camper at Higley Flow awakened to find the earth undulating...and the earth beneath him stunk! In the first place, there shouldn't have been earth beneath him, stinky or not, because he was on his dock which had been surrounded by water the night before. But now his dock was on about an acre of dry land, and the land was floating! How was he going to tell this one to his buddies? At first, nobody believed him, until they saw it for themselves. The following year, another island was born, bobbing and bubbling slowly up to the surface like a sinking ship scene in

Courtesy of *Adirondack Album—Volume Two* by Barney Fowler

Photo of a "floating island"

reverse. Year after year, for thirty years, floating islands kept surfacing from the depths of the reservoir.

The area encompassing Higley Flow centuries ago was a shallow pond or small lake that eventually filled in with vegetation that was so dense that it became a swamp. But the swamp had nothing to secure itself to— rather than attaching to bedrock (which there wasn't any of), it rested unstably on a bed of loose glacial sand. The vegetation couldn't take root and grow, so the only thing holding the swampland onto the sandy bottom of the river was gravity. It wouldn't take much stirring of the water to dislodge portions of such swampland, one by one, and send them to the surface. When the dam was created by the power company in 1912, the swampy area was inundated by turbulent waters, and it was that singular act that set the phenomenon into motion.

Now that the physics of the phenomenon were understood, nearby residents and those operating the dams simply learned to adjust and work around their floating islands—towing or pushing the smaller islands into the current where they would drift over the dam and disintegrate into the murky waters of the Raquette River. That seemed to work for three decades, until the last three islands were born. Like a mother giving birth to her tenth child, the last three were much bigger than the little 'practice' ones that came before them. And, to make it

114

even more interesting, the largest of them all was covered with "pitcher plants," a carnivorous plant that traps and eats bugs!

At any rate, the final three floating islands were far too large to fit over the power company's dam, and that meant trouble. It was time to come up with a new plan. Setting the islands on fire, soaked with gasoline and oil (before the days of stiff environmental fines), did nothing but pollute the air, earth, and water. Weighing the island down with heavy boulders to make them sink back to where they came from didn't work either, because the boulders sank through the flimsy mass of sod and tangled root, leaving the floating islands pock-marked but still afloat. Dynamite only succeeded in blasting tiny tunnels through the tortured islands, which, by this time, must have been a sight to see—burnt, pock-marked, and gouged.

Then in 1942, someone came up with a brilliant idea. If they waited till the dead of winter when the three remaining islands were frozen solid, they could saw them up into smaller islands that would fit through the dam. But where, in 1942, would you find a saw big enough to cut through fifteen feet of soil and debris? The contractor who was awarded the job of sawing the islands into pieces was Charles Waggamen, so it was his task to find the "wonder saw." And find it he did—in one Howard Mason's barn! It was an old, rusty drag saw with a one-cylinder engine that was still workable. Waggamen bought it for $125. By welding two parts of the saw together, it created twelve feet of cutting edge...and a pretty funny looking saw. Waggaman told curious onlookers that it was called an "Island Saw."

And so it was that in the winter of 1942, the floating island dispersion project began in full swing. The old saw worked exceedingly well, and the islands were cut into squares. Then a hole was cut through the center of each square, and a log, tied around the middle, was dropped through the hole, so that when it was tugged on, it would float back up to the underside of the island and lay flat against it (rather than shooting back up through the hole). This method of "hooking" the islands permitted them to then be towed by shore-based trucks. In spring of 1943, the last of the sliced-up floating island pieces went over the dam, causing a lot of extra work for a number of days for river mills downstream, but they had all been informed of the event and were well-prepared. And now you know...the rest of the story.

Strange Stone Carvings

Rossie

Spragueville is a small hamlet of the town of Rossie on the border of St. Lawrence and Jefferson Counties. Originally, the crossroads settlement was called Sprague's Corners, named after one of its earliest settlers. The population of Sprague's Corners in the late 1600s was zero. In fact, nobody settled in the Rossie area until the early 1800s. That's why an engraved boulder discovered by Spragueville's earliest settlers in the 1820s is still an enigma. It was reported for the first time in the turn-of-the-century authoritative compilation, *History of St. Lawrence County* by Gates Curtis. In a sense, it was date-stamped by someone in a primitive manner with the year "1671" being carved into limestone on a rocky knoll on the Stammer Road near Spragueville. According to LaRue's *St. Lawrence County Almanac*, the numbers 1-6-7-1 were carved into the stone about an inch deep, and the five-inch-tall numbers are well-formed. Unfortunately for future generations, several adjacent etchings in limestone at the same location have weathered away to the point that they are currently impossible to decipher.

The most widely-accepted explanation for the carvings is that they were left by a group of early pioneers from a fort in Kingston, Ontario—across the river—who explored this region long ago but did not settle here. This theory seems to make sense, because not too far away from the carvings, according to LaRue, is a twelve-foot-deep pit with a drainage ditch leading away from it. It's believed that the pioneers from Ontario discovered the same pit and dug a drainage ditch leading from it so they could drain the water out in anticipation of finding gold, silver, and other precious metals. Their hard work was in vain, however. All they actually found in the bottom of the pit were chunks of wood and debris. Realizing that the only gold in these hills was "fool's gold," or pyrite, which has the appearance of real gold but holds no value whatsoever, they returned to their fort, leaving the area to be uninhabited for another 130-odd years.

Thompson Park Vortex

Watertown

Northern New York boasts its very own "mysterious place" in *Sacred Sites: A Guidebook to Sacred Centers and Mysterious Places.* Smack in the center of the city of Watertown is the Thompson Park Nature Conservancy and its alleged "invisible doorway into other worlds," also known as a portal, vortex, or a phenomenon called "light-lines." I've written of other locations believed to contain such gateways, and usually they seem to be located on sacred sites such as Indian burial grounds, possibly because the Native American seers (i.e. shamans) were able to sense gateways in which their dead could more easily and quickly cross over and gain access to the Great Spirit. Often places that are haunted by a number of ghosts are also believed to contain portals, such as Spanky's Diner in Massena where the ghosts themselves told psychic investigators that Spanky's was like a Grand Central Station for spirits to come and go at ease—primarily in the basement so as not to disturb the dining public! Perhaps one of the most famous possible portals is the Bermuda Triangle, known for its many past disappearances of ships and aircraft. Thankfully, that door seems to be closed and locked at least for now.

Nobody knows for certain what causes these breaches into other dimensions; although some believe they were created because of a high number of tragic deaths or burials in one spot—maybe so many souls were leaving at once that it left a permanent scar (or open wound) in the thin veil between worlds. Another theory, the one mentioned in *Sacred Sites*, is that these doorways exist where glaciers imprinted unusual energy into the earth in objects such as the stone walls at Thompson Park, which then absorbed and now continually release the unusual energy back into the atmosphere.

The particulars of the paranormal incidents which allegedly have occurred at Thompson Park because of its vortex were reported, not only in the aforementioned book, but also in two regional newspapers, the *Watertown Daily Times* and the *Syracuse Post-Standard*; and a number of websites briefly mention the Park and its mystical gateway. The story goes that several visitors to Thompson Park have vanished into thin air (and reappeared moments later elsewhere). The first incident which received publicity occurred in the mid-seventies when a man disappeared in plain site as he walked away from the group he was with. A short time later, as the group was frantically searching for him, he reappeared behind them, telling them he'd been looking for them.

A few years later, it happened again to one of the members of the original group whose students said she had vanished before their eyes. Those two incidents are solely responsible for the rumors of the Park having a portal in its midst, which is said to be in a grove of trees near an exercise course, golf course, and swimming pool. Whether it does have a portal or not is anyone's guess, but the many people who have worked there or visited in search of something paranormal are adamant that they've noticed nothing out of the ordinary. Then again, those who were involved in the two earlier incidents are just as adamant that there is something paranormal going on.

Yes, you can hear dogs howling all the time at the Park, especially near the alleged portal, but the city dog pound is located adjacent to the property. And reports of disembodied voices are common (though a little more eerie sounding) in places where there are hills and especially stone fences. But maybe there really is someone calling out from one dimension to another, if a portal does exist there. I contacted the Park in 2000, when I was writing my first book to ask if they had any inside information, and the only response I received came from a maintenance employee who said he'd never seen or heard anything in all his time there, but he was kind enough to send copies of the newspaper articles cited above. If anyone has further information, I'd love to include an update on the vortex in a future volume.

Surprising Snippets

Before Internet Dating

Raquette Lake

These days, it's not uncommon to find a marriage partner online through web sites like Match.com, Matchmaker.com, and Date.com. In fact, online dating has become a trendy service, allowing potential love interests to communicate with each other from afar—even overseas—before ever meeting in person. To give you an idea of the rising popularity of this type of courtship in modern society, when Match.com first started up in 1995, about sixty-thousand people joined that first year. Today, Match.com now boasts more than fifteen million members. That's a lot of potential love interests to choose from! Suffice it to say, it's never been easier to find a mate. But before the advent of the Internet, cupid had to be a little more creative.

An article taken from *The Elizabethtown Post* in Essex County on April 24, 1890, told of a young woman whose umbrella traveled across the globe and landed in the hands of a man she didn't know, but whom she would one day marry. It said:

"While working in an umbrella factory in Sheffield, England, about three years ago, Miss Anna Hodgson wrote her name and address on an umbrella which she had just completed. The result brought about by this careless action is quite romantic. Along with hundreds of others, the umbrella was shipped to this country. At New York is was sold to a merchant, and finally reached Long Lake, Hamilton County, and was purchased by a young man named Jerome Wood. Some weeks passed before he noticed the name on its interior. Then he wrote to the young woman whose address was on the umbrella. She answered. The correspondence, thus strangely started, lasted until her departure for this country. She took up residence in Troy as a house-keeper for her brother. After some time she went to Palmer's Falls, thence to Raquette Lake, where she was employed during the summer at The Antlers. Mr. Wood was employed at the lake by W.W. Durant, and it was there that the lady and gentleman first met. At Luzerne the past week, Miss Hodges and Mr. Wood were made one. So much for the umbrella romance."

Thousand Island Dressing

Clayton

We've all heard the tragic tale of Boldt Castle—how hotel magnate George C. Boldt began construction of a grand castle for his wife on an island he reportedly reshaped to match it's new name, Heart Island. Valentine's Day 1904 was the day Boldt planned to present the castle to his wife Louise as a testament to his love for her, but she died unexpectedly in January, leaving George Boldt devastated...and with no desire to finish his masterpiece. When word of Louise's passing reached George, he ordered all construction stopped—three hundred people put down their tools that day and left the island; and George Boldt never returned. The castle remained abandoned, and open to vandals and the elements, for seventy-three years. In 1977, the Thousand Islands Bridge Authority acquired the property and has since put millions of dollars into restoring the castle and its surrounding structures on Heart Island, making it one of the most famous and favored tourist and school group attractions in the region. That's why "Boldt Castle" immediately comes to mind for most people when they think about the Thousand Islands. And George Boldt was also somewhat responsible for another famous item that often comes to mind when you think about the Thousand Islands...Thousand Island Dressing.

Sophia LaLonde of Clayton created a salad dressing which she served to appreciative dinner guests of her husband, George Jr., a popular fishing guide in the early 1900s. The rich and famous came from afar to relax in the Thousand Islands region each year back then, and one day a prominent New York City stage actress named May Irwin arrived with her husband. Like Sophia, Ms. Irwin was a good cook, as well, and had published her own cookbook. She loved the dressing and asked George for the recipe from his wife. Sophia could not have known the outcome of sharing her recipe that day when she kindly obliged, giving both the actress and the woman whose family owned the hotel the actress was staying at, Ms. Ella Bertrand of the Herald Hotel in Clayton, the recipe. From then on, Ms. Bertrand included the dressing in her menu for customers at the hotel, which was renamed the Thousand Islands Inn in 1972. But the big break didn't come until Ms. Irwin returned to New York City and gave the recipe to her dear friend—none other than George C. Boldt, owner of the famous Waldorf-Astoria Hotel in New York City; the Bellview Stratford Hotel in Philadelphia, Pennsylvania; and, of course, the aforementioned Boldt Castle on Heart Island.

Boldt directed his famous maître d'hôtel, Oscar Tschirky, best known as "Oscar of the Waldorf," to put the dressing on the Waldorf-Astoria's hotel menu, and that's when Thousand Island Dressing soared to fame. It was created by a humble housewife, named "Thousand Island" by the well-known stage actress who first asked for the recipe and shared it with friends, and introduced to the public at large by a hotel magnate (and his famous maître d') with ties to the North Country. The rest, as they say, is history.

By 1912, the Thousand Island Dressing recipe was found in cookbooks and publications, and it had become known around the world. Today, many leading fast food restaurants use a version of Thousand Island Dressing on some of their sandwiches, and many major dressing manufacturers have their own brand of Thousand Island Dressing. But if you want to taste the original recipe created by Sophia LaLonde a hundred years ago, you can purchase a bottle at the Thousand Islands Inn in Clayton or order it from their website. Thousand Island Dressing is the official house dressing at the inn, which was licensed by the state in 1990 to package the original recipe for sale.

Acknowledgements

I'd like to thank my publisher, Rob Igoe of North Country Books, along with his right-hand man, Zach Steffen, for their encouragement and understanding.

Many thanks to all who contributed information for stories, especially Phillip Creighton and the rest of his Shadow Chasers; Marc and Sarah Spicer; and Steve, Mary, Brian, Debbie, Danny, and Donna.

Special acknowledgements go to Bob LaRue and the late Barney Fowler, two great fellow researchers and authors. Bob is the author of the popular *St. Lawrence County Almanac* series; while Barney was the author of the wonderful *Adirondack Album* series. I gleaned much information and a number of leads from both men's works, and several of Mr. Fowler's photographs grace the pages of this book, thanks to his publisher, Bob Kosineski of Benchemark Printing.

As always, I thank my parents, Tom and Jean Dishaw; my siblings, Chris Walker, Cindy (CJ) Barry, and Tom Dishaw; and my girls— Michelle, Jamie, Katie, and Nikki—for their continued support. I know I told them just one more book, and that was five books ago...

The most gratitude this time around goes to Leland Farnsworth, my better half. He's the one who keeps me on track, does the cooking, fields the phone calls, entertains Nikki (six years old), and forbids me to procrastinate (even when I moan and complain and carry on)—all to make sure I get a book written on schedule.

Thank you all so much.

Bibliography

Books

Curtis, Gates, ed. *History of St. Lawrence County, New York: Our County and its People.* Salem, MA: Higgison Book Co., reprint of 1894 edition.

Dumas, Eleanor and Nina. *History of Massena, the Orphan Town.* Massena, NY: Published by the authors, 1977.

Everts, H.L. and J.M. Holcomb, *History of St. Lawrence County, New York.* Syracuse, NY: D. Mason & Company, 1878.

Fowler, Barney. *Adirondack Album.* Schenectady, NY: Outdoor Associates, 1982 (reprint).

——*Adirondack Album—Volume Two.* Schenectady, NY: Outdoor Associates, 1974.

Frank, Joseph. *Sacred Sites: A Guidebook to Sacred Centers and Mysterious Places.* Woodbury, MN: Llewellyn Publications, 1992.

LaRue, Robert J. *St. Lawrence County Almanac—1st Edition Vignettes.* Syracuse, NY: Peerless Press, Inc., 1996.

——*St. Lawrence County Almanac—2nd Edition Vignettes.* Syracuse, NY: Peerless Press, Inc., 1997.

——*St. Lawrence County Almanac—Volume 4—Photo Edition.* Syracuse, NY: Peerless Press, Inc., 2000.

Revai, Cheri. *Haunted Northern New York*. Utica, NY: North Country Books, Inc., 2002.

———*More Haunted Northern New York*. Utica, NY: North Country Books, Inc., 2003.

———*Still More Haunted Northern New York*. Utica, NY: North Country Books, Inc., 2004.

———*Haunted New York: Ghosts & Strange Phenomena of the Empire State*. Mechanicsburg, PA: Stackpole Books, Inc., 2005.

Seaver, Frederick J. *Historical Sketches of Franklin County and Its Several Towns, With Many Short Biographies*. Albany: JB Lyon Company, 1918.

The American Heritage College Dictionary—Third Edition. Boston, New York: Houghton Mifflin Company, 2000.

Online Sources

"Adirondack Lives," Adirondack Museum. Retrieved 26 July 2006.
www.adirondackhistory.org/

"Adirondack Wolves," Go Back to the Basics. Retrieved 25 July 2006.
www.gobacktothebasics.com/information_and_stories_on_the_adiron-
dack_wolf.htm

"An Umbrella Romance," News from Hamilton County, NY. Retrieved
16 August 2006. www.rootsweb.com/~nyhamilt/misc/Newspapers2.html

"Boldt Castle," 1000 Islands. Retrieved 25 July 2006.
http://www.1000islands.com/castle/

"Centenarians," Gerontology Research Group. Retrieved 1 June 2006.
www.grg.org/calment.html

"Comments," HaloScan.com. Retrieved 18 July 2006.
www.haloscan.com/comments/levi9909/111334051440733869/

"Delina Filkins," Wikipedia, the free encyclopedia. Retrieved 1 June 2006.
http://en.wikipedia.org/wiki/Delina_Filkins

Dixon, Miss Poppy. "Blood Libel," Blood Libel: Racism and the Fear of
Sex in the Pro-life Movement. Retrieved 26 July 2006.
www.postfun.com/pfp/features/98/oct/bloodlibel.html

"Do Earthquakes Occur in New York State?" Earthquakes and
Earthquake Engineering... Retrieved 18 July 2006.
http://mceer.buffalo.edu/infoService/faqs/eqlist.asp

"Earthquakes in the Charlevoix-Kamouraska Seismic Zone," USGS Earthquake Hazards Program: Tectonic Summary: Gaspe Peninsula, Canada. Retrieved 18 July 2006. http://neic.usgs.gov/neis/eq_depot/2005/eq_050306/neic_vhan_ts.html

Eckler, A. Ross. "109 Year Old (1924) Mohawk Valley Woman," Roots Web. Retrieved 1 June 2006. www.rootsweb.com/~nyherkim/stark/109lady.html

"Eighteen Hundred and Froze to Death—The Year There was No Summer," Weather Doctor's Weather People and History. Retrieved 25 July 2006. www.islandnet.com/~see/weather/history/1816.htm

Flynn, Andy. "Artifact: Photo of Jacques Suzanne, the 'Great Explorer,'" Adirondack Attic. Retrieved 26 July 2006. http://adkattic.blogspot.com/2006/03/artifact-photo-of-jacques-suzanne.html

"Ghost Story of Old Stands Up to Tests of Time," Press-Republican Online. Retrieved 17 July 2006. http://archive.pressrepublican.com/Archive/2001/08_2001/08122001gl.htm

"Gray Wolf Fact Sheet," New York State Department of Environmental Conservation. Retrieved 25 July 2006. www.dec.state.ny.us/website/dfwmr/wildlife/endspec/grwofs.html

"Higley Flow State Park," New York State Parks. Retrieved 27 July 2006. http://nysparks.state.ny.us/parks/print.asp?parkID=144

"Higley Flow State Park," Wikipedia, the free encyclopedia. Retrieved 27 July 2006. http://en.wikipedia.org/wiki/Higley_Flow_State_Park

"History—Online Dating," M/Cyclopedia of New Media. Retrieved 17 August 2006. http://wiki.media-culture.org.au/index.php/Online_Dating

"History of Altamont, New York," History of Altamont, New York. Retrieved 16 August 2006. www.history.rays-place.com/ny/altamont-ny.htm

"How did Thousand Island Dressing get its name?" Ask Yahoo. Retrieved 16 August 2006. http://ask.yahoo.com/20031218.html

"Lake Ontario," Ontario Lake Monsters. Retrieved 14 July 2006. www.parasearchers.org/

Landau, Joel. "Former Dean Leaves Ghostly Legacy," The Daily Targum (Posted 10/31/02). Retrieved 25 July 2006. www.dailytargum.com

"Litchfield Castle," Dupont Castle. Retrieved 23 June 2006. www.dupontcastle.com/castles/litchfie.htm

"Litchfield's Chateau Monument to Tenacity," Watertown Daily Times (online). Retrieved 22 June 2006. www.wdt.net

Mellon, Peter. "The Boats of George C. Boldt," Bolts Boats. Retrieved 16 August 2006. www.acbm.us/bolt-boats.htm

"New York—Higley Flow State Park," Wildernet—Higley Flow State Park. Retrieved 27 July 2006. www.wildernet.com/pages/area.cfm?areaID=NYSPHF&CU_ID=1

"News from Hamilton County, NY," Roots Web. Retrieved 16 August 2006. www.rootsweb.com/~nyhamilt/misc/Newspapers2.html

"Noah John Rondeau," Adirondack Park. Retrieved 25 July 2006. www.adirondack-park.net/history/noah.john.rondeau.html

Nutt, Amy Ellis. "Mabel Smith's Vision Now Douglass Residential College," (blog) New Jersey Online. Retrieved 25 July 2006. www.nj.com/weblogs/print.ssf?/mtlogs/njo_writers/archives/print120293.html

"Of Earthquakes and Explosions," Rensselaer Magazine: Spring 2006: Mail. Retrieved 18 July 2006. www.rpi.edu/dept/metasite/news/magazine/spring2006/mail.html

Revetta, Frank. The Potsdam Seismic Network and Earthquakes in Northern New York. Retrieved 18 July 2006. http://gsa.confex.com/gsa/2006NE/finalprogram/abstract_100149.htm

"Rossie, New York: Information," Answers.com. Retrieved 25 July 2006. www.answers.com/rossie%20new%20york

"Sea Serpents," Akwesasne Phoenix. Retrieved 24 July 2006.
www.akwesasnephoenix.com/serpent1.html

"Skull & Bones Society," Skull and Bones, The Yale Secret Society.
Retrieved 25 July 2006.
www.skullandbones.org/articles/skullandbones.htm

"Skull and Bones," Skull and Bones—Wikipedia, the free encyclopedia.
Retrieved 14 July 2006. http://en.wikipedia.org/wiki/Skull_and_Bones

Stith, Barbara. "Opening the Door to Mystery, April 12, 1993" The Post-
Standard (online). Retrieved 22 June 2006. www.syracuse.com

"Stories and Legends," Ausable Chasm—Chasm. Retrieved 17 July 2006.
http://ausablechasm.com/stories.htm

"The Bellevue-Stratford Hotel," Wikipedia, the free encyclopedia. Retrieved
16 August 2006. http://en.wikipedia.org/wiki/The_Bellevue_Stratford_Hotel

"The BrightSide on Raquette," BrightSide on Raquette. Retrieved 11
August 2006. www.brightsideonraquette.com

"The History of Deer Island," New Ruins—Deer Island Discovery Site.
Retrieved 18 August 2006.
http://www.newruins.com/Discover_di/main.html

"The Massena Blood Libel," The American Jewish Historical Society
(AJHS). Retrieved 25 July 2006. www.ajhs.org/publications/chapters/chap-
ter.cfm?documentID=288

"The Order of Skull and Bones," The Order of Skull and Bones—
Crystalinks. Retrieved 25 July 2006.
www.crystalinks.com/skullbones.html

"Thousand Island Dressing," 1000 Islands. Retrieved 16 August 2006.
www.1000islands.com/inn/dressing.htm

"Thousand Island dressing," Wikipedia, the free encyclopedia. Retrieved 16 August 2006. http://en.wikipedia.org/wiki/Thousand_Island_dressing

"TIME Magazine Archive Article—Red Mass—Oct. 15, 1928," Time Archive 1923 to the Present. Retrieved 26 July 2006. http://time-proxy.yaga.com/time/archive/preview/0,10987,731996,00.html

About the Author

Photo by Creative Imaging, Watertown

Author, Cheri Revai

Cheri Revai is a mother of four, a secretary, and the author of the best-selling *Haunted Northern New York, More Haunted Northern New York*, and *Still More Haunted Northern New York*; as well as *Haunted Massachusetts: Ghosts & Strange Phenomena of the Bay State, Haunted New York: Ghosts & Strange Phenomena of the Empire State*, and *Haunted Connecticut: Ghosts & Strange Phenomena of the Constitution State*. She is a North Country native who enjoys travel, research, and history. She resides in Massena with her family and a menagerie of pets.